Contents

Foreword	*page*	4
Introduction		5
1.	How the tax system fits together	6
2.	The poor and the rich	8
3.	What has happened to the tax system since 1979?	11
4.	An international comparison	14
5.	The structure of income tax rates	16
6.	Income tax allowances	18
7.	Employee national insurance contributions	21
8.	Taxation of husband and wife: now and 1990	23
9.	Taxation of husband and wife: alternatives	25
10.	Tax and social security	28
11.	Tax and social security: reforms	30
12.	How investment income and capital gains are taxed now	33
13.	Fundamental reforms to the taxation of investment income	36
14.	Reforms within a hybrid tax system	38
15.	Taxing wealth and inheritance	40
16.	Value Added Tax	42
17.	Drinking, driving and smoking	44
18.	Rates, the Poll Tax and local income tax	46
19.	Taxing companies	49
20.	A strategy for reform	52
Where to find out more		56
Notes		60
Index		63

Foreword

Today the tax system is more visible, and, its structure more a live topic of debate, than it has been at any other time in recent years. The 'water-shed' Budget of March 1988, with its abolition of all but one of the higher tax rates and its other generous tax cuts for the better-off, has raised in more people's minds than ever before questions about the overall impact of the tax system in this country. And the Government's proposals to introduce a 'community charge', or poll tax, have highlighted similar issues of redistributive justice.

So taxation and tax reform have been placed firmly on the political agenda over the past year. CPAG therefore asked John Hills – an expert in the field, and a member of CPAG's Executive Committee – to write *Changing Tax* as a contribution to the growing public debate.

How taxation policy might be changed to create a more rational and redistributive tax system has always been a key area of concern for CPAG. In particular, we have, over the years, submitted annual pre-Budget Memoranda to the Chancellor of the Exchequer, analysing the impact of taxation on different income groups and setting out reasoned proposals for change. We have been interested in both 'vertical' and 'horizontal' redistribution – the structure of the tax system and its effects on people with different levels of income and with different family commitments.

Our major area of interest has always, of course, been low income families with children. But from this perspective we have commented – both in our Budget Memos and in other documents – on direct and indirect taxes, national insurance contributions, forms of local taxation and the interaction between the social security and tax systems. *Changing Tax* brings together these various areas of concern in one publication – and adds others of which the author also has in-depth knowledge. With the growing complexity of benefits and fiscal measures, it is not possible to isolate the discussion of particular policies for helping families and the poor from the chosen forms of financing them.

CPAG's central concerns in taxation policy are two-fold. First comes *fairness*. While some would argue that 'fairness' involves everyone paying the same amount (as will be the case for the majority of the population under the poll tax), most would not. CPAG has always argued for a more progressive tax system, which takes a higher proportionate share of the incomes (and capital) of the better-off than of the worse-off. This view is in line with the general opinion in all political parties over the last decade – and, indeed, was endorsed by the general public in recent polls showing that two out of three thought the 1988 Budget unfair and that an even higher proportion disagreed with the introduction of a poll tax.

But there are also other issues involved in 'fair' taxation. CPAG has always argued for a tax and benefits system which gives greater recognition to the lower 'taxable capacity' of families with children, who have higher needs than those without children at whatever level of income.

And we have argued too for other important considerations to be taken into account – such as fairness in the treatment of men and women, which we believe should lead to independent taxation of individuals, regardless of gender or marital status. Unfortunately, recent developments in tax policy under this and the last two governments since 1979 have for the most part been moving towards a less fair system in each of these three areas of CPAG's concern – as John Hills' book clearly demonstrates.

The second, and perhaps most basic, reason why CPAG must be interested in a re-examination of options for reforming the tax system is *funding*. Those who advocate more generous levels of benefits or more adequate public services are always asked where the money will come from. The chosen methods of financing improvements must be seen as fairer and more rational in order for these measures themselves to be widely accepted as fair and rational.

John Hills comes clearly to two conclusions. One is that it *is* possible to devise a more progressive tax system which will finance a package of more generous benefit levels, whilst at the same time raising the same amount of revenue for other spending. The second is that it is not possible to do this merely by looking longingly at the incomes of the very few extremely rich individuals in this country or by 'tinkering' in minor ways with the existing tax structure; but there *is* enormous scope for achieving change, and attracting broad support for it, if a more comprehensive re-structuring is considered.

We hope that this publication will both add to the growing body of knowledge about the operation of the existing tax system and contribute to the growing public debate about constructive alternatives to it.

Fran Bennett
Director
Child Poverty Action Group
October 1988

CHANGING TAX

How the tax system works
and how to change it

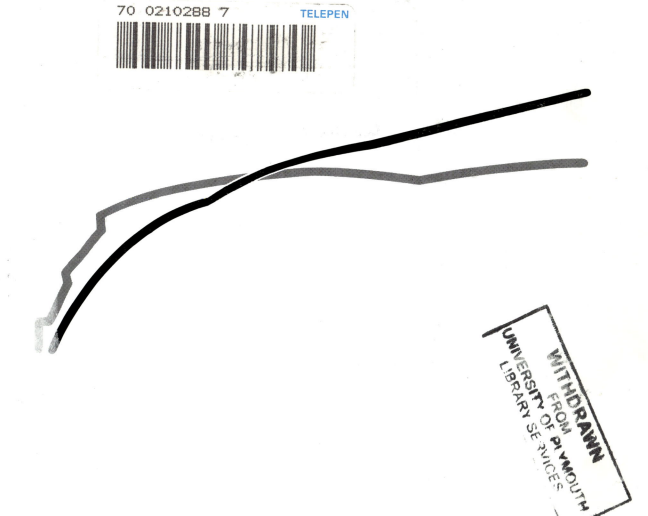

JOHN HILLS

Acknowledgements

I am very grateful to CPAG for their help and encouragement in producing this book, especially Julia Lewis and Peter Ridpath, and to Calvert's for their rapid and imaginative work in turning the typescript into the finished product. Thanks are due to Stephen Smith for help with the sections on indirect taxes, and to Fran Bennett, Mervyn King, Carey Oppenheim and David Piachaud for many helpful comments and suggested improvements to earlier drafts. My colleagues at LSE displayed great forbearance as the spare time in which this was supposed to be written encroached into the time of the Welfare State Programme, supported by the Suntory-Toyota International Centre for Economics and Related Disciplines. Finally, I owe a particular debt to Tony Atkinson and Holly Sutherland who not only made many invaluable comments on the draft, but also made the whole exercise possible through the construction of their model of the tax and benefit systems, which could not have been more friendly than it was to this user.

© CPAG Limited 1988
1–5 Bath Street, London EC1V 9PY

British Library Cataloguing in Publication Data
Hills, John
   Changing tax: how the tax system works and
   how to change it
   1. Great Britain. Taxation
   I. Title
   336.2'00941

ISBN 0-946744-14-9

Designed, typeset and printed by
Calvert's Press (TU) Workers' Co-operative
31–39 Redchurch Street, London E2 7DJ

Introduction

The tax system is simultaneously very important to people's lives and also mysterious and misunderstood in its operation. While the level of public debate has improved greatly in recent years, discussion of tax changes remains dominated by experts and by the information provided by the Government. It is still possible for a Budget like that of 1988 to be popularly presented as a 'tax-cutting' Budget, even though its effects were projected by the Treasury to leave the share of national income taken in tax virtually unchanged. There were indeed tax cuts for some, but there were also far less visible forces resulting in an equivalent increase in the tax burden for others. In recent years the combination of these forces with more explicit changes has produced a major *shift* in the tax burden, rather than the overall fall popularly supposed to have occurred.

Part of the intention of this book is to provide a straightforward description of how the tax system operates, for people without any specialist knowledge or background, and to act as an introduction to the literature on the subject. Each of the sections which follows is intended to provide a relatively self-contained briefing on the particular topic which it concerns.

The book has two further objectives. One is to answer the question posed whenever an organisation like the Child Poverty Action Group (CPAG) proposes improvements to the benefit system: where does the money come from? In particular, can more money be raised from taxation without raising tax rates to levels which provoke 'avoidance' and 'evasion' and which can damage the operation of the economy? Its second objective is to examine each component of the system to see how its operation could be made more progressive – that is, shift the tax burden from those on lower incomes towards those on higher ones – while simultaneously removing anomalies and inconsistencies in its existing structure.

It does not set out to make the philosophical case for a more equitable distribution of the country's resources; there is already plenty of material available for those who still need to be convinced. Its aim is, rather, to provide a manual for those who want to achieve that aim.

Finally, the book makes no attempt to provide an examination of macro-economic management. One argument which has been put forward in favour of the distributional strategy which has been followed since 1979 (some of the consequences of which are outlined in Section 2) is that, although those on lower incomes are receiving a declining share of the national cake, the size of the cake is growing more rapidly than hitherto, making up for their losses. From the forecasts made at the time of the 1988 Budget, the country's growth rate between 1979 and 1988 comes to 2% per year, averaging over the slump of the first years and the subsequent recovery.[1] This compares with a growth rate of 2.6% per year over the period 1948-1979 during which inequalities in the distribution of income were declining (see Figure 2a). It is not even any higher than the 2% per year growth over the period 1974-1979 when the economy was coping with the oil price shock, rather than benefiting from North Sea oil. The burden of proof in the argument as to whether the strategy of inequality will bring long-term benefits even to those who have lost out in the last decade lies with its proponents.

The first four sections provide the background for the rest of the book, giving an overview of the tax system (Section 1), information about trends in the distribution of income (Section 2), an analysis of the cumulative effect of the tax changes over the last decade (Section 3) and a brief comparison of Britain's tax structure with that in other countries (Section 4). The following sections examine different aspects of the tax system and possibilities for their reform, including: the structure of direct taxes (Sections 5, 6 and 7); the tax treatment of husband and wife (Sections 8 and 9); the relationship between tax and social security (Sections 10 and 11); the taxation of investment income and capital gains (Sections 12, 13 and 14); wealth and inheritance taxes (Section 15); indirect taxes (Sections 16 and 17); local taxation (Section 18); and taxes on companies (Section 19). Section 20 shows how some of the ideas in the rest of the book could be brought together into a package of progressive reforms. A final section gives a guide to further reading on each of the topics covered by the book. Technical terms are defined when they first appear and are referenced in the index.

Many of the results of the sections dealing with possible reforms to the direct tax system showing their effects on distribution and on the revenue received by the government, have been produced using the microcomputer model of the tax and benefit system, TAXMOD.[2] This model, designed and written at the London School of Economics by A.B. Atkinson and Holly Sutherland, is an invaluable tool for the kind of analysis presented here. It shows the results of reforms, taking account of the many complex interactions between different parts of the tax and benefit system and shows how they would affect a large representative sample of the population (not a handful of supposedly 'typical', but usually in fact rather atypical, hypothetical families). It is important to note, however, that the model does not show the behavioural changes which might result from changes to the tax structure. What it shows are 'first round' effects of tax and benefit changes, not the knock-on effects which would ripple through the economy as a whole. The tables and figures drawn from the model are marked with the TAXMOD logo.

One of the great advantages of recent improvements in microcomputer technology is that models like TAXMOD (which is available at cost price from the Suntory-Toyota International Centre for Economics and Related Disciplines, LSE, 10 Portugal Street, London WC2A 2HD) can be used by people outside the confines of the Treasury and the Inland Revenue. The analysis of tax reform is no longer just a spectator sport.

John Hills
September 1988

1. How the tax system fits together

In the tax year starting in April 1988 ('1988-89') the Government planned to raise £173 billion in tax revenue, 38% of Britain's national income.[1] The way this is broken down between the various taxes is shown in the table below which is divided into two parts. **Direct taxes,** which depend on the circumstances – mostly the incomes or profits – of individual taxpayers or companies, account for more than half the total, with **Income Tax** the single biggest contributor. **Indirect taxes** are charged on particular kinds of spending regardless of the personal circumstances of those doing the spending; the most important of these is **Value Added Tax** (VAT).

Tax revenues 1988-89 (Budget forecast)

	£ BILLION
Direct Taxes	
Income Tax	42.1
National Insurance Contributions	31.6
Corporation Tax	17.3
Capital taxes	4.7
Other (mainly North Sea)	2.6
	98.3
Indirect taxes	
Value Added Tax	26.2
Rates	19.0
Excise Duties	17.9
Other (eg, car tax, stamp duties customs, etc.)	11.4
	74.5

SOURCE: *Financial Statement and Budget Report 1988* (the 'Red Book')

Income Tax (discussed in detail in Sections 5 to 14) not only remains the most important tax in revenue-raising terms but is also the most important in determining the distributional effects of the tax system – that is, how people at different income levels are affected – as the amounts charged can be tailored to individual circumstances.

The tax is charged on all regular forms of income – wages, salaries, interest, dividends, the profits of the self-employed, rent received – and some 'benefits in kind' like the use of a company car. It is not applied to capital gains (but Capital Gains Tax is now affected by people's Income Tax position – see below). Since 1963 it has not applied to owner occupiers' 'imputed rents' (the cash equivalent of the value of living in their homes rent-free).

The amount of tax depends on total income from all sources over the whole year. For people with earnings, the tax due is worked out by their employer and is withheld from their wages or salary each week, or monthly under the **Pay As You Earn** (PAYE) system. For many kinds of investment income, like bank or building society interest or dividends, the investor also receives a **net** amount (that is, one from which a standard tax charge has been deducted 'at source').

These arrangements mean that most people auto-matically pay the right amount of tax without the Inland Revenue (which collects Income Tax) having to have any direct contact with them. Only a minority of taxpayers, those with relatively complicated affairs, have to complete a **tax return** giving details of their income once the tax year has ended so that the Inland Revenue can work out their final tax bill. In most other countries a much greater proportion of taxpayers have to go through this process – in some cases, such as the USA, all taxpayers have to complete a tax return.

National Insurance Contributions (NICs) are discussed in Sections 7 (employee contributions) and 19 (contributions by employers and the self-employed). They are notionally a payment towards items like the state pension and Unemployment Benefit (the role of NICs in funding the National Health Service is very limited, despite popular belief to the contrary). Originally NICs were at a flat rate regardless of the size of an individual's earnings, but these days they are calculated as a percentage of earnings (with upper and lower limits which are described in Section 7).

As NICs theoretically contribute towards benefits which an individual might receive later, they are not always classed as a tax. However, the link between contributions and benefits is rather obscure (although important in the case of earnings-related pensions), and governments treat the revenue from them in the same way as any other tax: the National Insurance 'Fund' into which contributions are paid is more of an accounting device than a reality.

Corporation Tax (see Section 19) is charged on the profits of incorporated businesses (unincorporated businesses pay Income Tax). Companies pay tax on their profits at the same rate (currently 35%), whether or not they 'retain' them for re-investment or 'distribute' them, as dividends to shareholders (but if they are distributed, some of the tax counts as an advance payment of the shareholders' Income Tax). Profits calculated for tax purposes are not exactly the same as those a company would show in its accounts. Before 1984, there was a substantial difference because of the generous allowances which companies could deduct when calculating taxable profits to encourage them to invest. These allowances were withdrawn, and the two measures of profits are now much closer.

Capital taxes have a fairly minor and declining role in the tax system. **Inheritance Tax** (see Section 15) now raises less than 3% of the amount raised by Income Tax; 40 years ago, the equivalent proportion was more than 12%.[2] The tax is levied from the estates of those who have died but, unlike its predecessor, **Capital Transfer Tax,** can be avoided by passing on wealth as lifetime gifts.

Capital Gains Tax (see Section 12) is charged on the difference between the prices at which an asset is bought and sold. It is not applied to owner-occupied houses, nor to gains simply reflecting the effects of inflation, and there is a generous annual tax-free allowance. In 1988 the rate of tax was tied to individuals' Income Tax rates, so that those with the highest incomes now pay more, but at the same time gains arising before 1982 were taken out of tax altogether.

Value Added Tax (see Section 16) is paid every time something is sold, apart from certain 'exempt' items like rent or 'zero-rated' items like some foods (see Section 16 for an explanation of the distinction). The tax is collected at each stage of production or distribution, but the amount paid eventually adds 15% to the final purchase price.

Rates (see Sections 18 and 19) are levied by local authorities on domestic residential and business properties in their area. The amount paid depends on the tax rate ('rate poundage') set by the authority and on the 'rateable value' assessed for each property. People living in more expensive houses therefore tend to pay more, but the amount they pay does not depend on their income (except to the extent that they might be entitled to help through Housing Benefit or Income Support). Domestic rates are to be abolished and replaced by the **Community Charge** (as it is officially called) or **Poll Tax** (as it is now almost universally known) in Scotland from April 1989 and in England and Wales from April 1990. Business rates will continue but will be taken out of the hands of individual local authorities and charged at a uniform national rate.

Excise Duties (see Section 17) on items like petrol, alcohol and tobacco are the most important of the other indirect taxes. They are calculated not only as a percentage of the price (that is, an 'ad valorem' rate), but also partly as a fixed ('specific') amount per pint of beer, bottle of wine, 20 cigarettes and so on. Excise duties are intended not only to raise money, but also to have 'regulatory' effects on behaviour such as discouraging smoking or drinking.

The combined effect of the taxes

One of the great problems of analysing tax systems is in working out their true **incidence**, that is who *really* pays them. Companies pay Corporation Tax on their profits, but may pass the tax on as higher prices, so that consumers rather than shareholders bear the burden of the tax in the end. The same could even be true of a tax like Income Tax: employers might have to pay higher *gross* (pre-tax) salaries in order to make sure that their employees end up with a particular level of *net* income (for instance, to compete with other employers abroad).

Assumptions therefore have to be made about the incidence of particular taxes. Those made below follow general convention: direct taxes like Income Tax and employee National Insurance Contributions are assumed to be borne by the people on whose income they are calculated; indirect taxes like VAT and Excise Duties are assumed to be borne by consumers. Such assumptions can be challenged, but they are probably reasonable when it comes to analysing *changes* in the tax structure. It does not appear, for instance, that the gross salaries of top earners have been *cut* in response to the cuts in the top rates of Income Tax in the last 10 years.

Using these incidence assumptions, Figures 1a and 1b show how taxes affected single people at different earnings levels in 1978-79 and 1988-89 respectively. The figures are based on answers to a Parliamentary Question[3] and are relatively simple examples of what would be paid by people with different earnings (without allowing for other income or for allowances like mortgage interest relief).

The Government only publishes estimates for the indirect tax burden for three of the earnings levels, based on national survey evidence for the relationship between spending patterns and disposable income (after direct taxes). The white parts of the columns show the total indirect tax burdens which would result for the other cases from extending the same assumed relationship[4] (although in these cases, there will be more uncertainty attached to the estimates).

The immediate surprise may be how little the *total* tax burden changed as a percentage of earnings between the tax years 1978-79 and 1988-89. A single person on average (men's) earnings would have paid 45.5% of earnings in these taxes in 1978-79; in 1988-89 the proportion was virtually unchanged at 45.6%. It is only at higher income levels than those shown that there have been any significant cuts in the tax burden.

Two things have changed however. The first is the balance between the different taxes. Income Tax is much less important than it was, while (employee) National Insurance Contributions, VAT and rates have all increased to compensate. Secondly, the **progressivity** of the structure – the extent to which people on higher incomes pay a larger proportion of their incomes in tax – has changed. Even in 1978-79, as earnings went from 0.5 to 3 times the average, the tax burden only rose from about 41% to about 51%. Ten years later the rise is from about 44% to 48%: the tax system has been tilted against those on low incomes in favour of the better off.

The series of measures which have created this 'tilt' against the poor are explored further in Section 3, which also examines what has happened to the population as a whole as a result of the changes (rather than just taking the 'hypothetical' examples in the diagrams, which may not be fully representative).

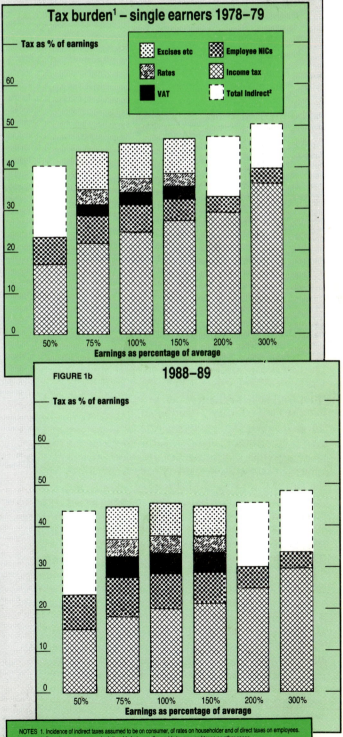

FIGURE 1a

Tax burden[1] – single earners 1978–79

Tax as % of earnings

Legend: Excises etc | Employee NICs | Rates | Income tax | VAT | Total Indirect[2]

Earnings as percentage of average: 50%, 75%, 100%, 150%, 200%, 300%

FIGURE 1b — **1988–89**

Tax as % of earnings

Earnings as percentage of average: 50%, 75%, 100%, 150%, 200%, 300%

NOTES 1. Incidence of indirect taxes assumed to be on consumer, of rates on householder and of direct taxes on employees.
2. Based on same assumed relationship between disposable income and taxes as other cases.

2. The poor and the rich

The tax system has not only to raise revenue but also to do this both *efficiently* (without heavy administrative costs or damaging the operation of the economy) and *equitably.* While equity is the major concern of this book, the *constraints* of efficiency have to be considered.

A key argument about the equity of taxation is about 'equality of sacrifice' – when raising taxes, the burden imposed by taking £1 from a high income is clearly less than that imposed by taking the same amount from a low income. More strongly, the burden imposed by taking 1% of the former will be less than that of taking 1% of the latter. Such arguments imply that the tax system should be **progressive** – ie, the *proportion* of income taken in tax should rise with income. As Figures 1a and 1b showed for hypothetical cases, much of the (limited) progressivity of the tax system in 1978-79 had gone by 1988-89.

A tax which takes a greater proportion of low than high incomes is **regressive.** The obvious example is the Poll Tax which will replace domestic rates (see Section 18). Under this new system, all adults in each area who are not entitled to rebates will pay the same cash amount. This will necessarily be a greater proportion of low than of high incomes.

Finally, a tax which takes the same proportion of all incomes is **proportional.** One complication of tax analysis is that taxes can be progressive over one income range but proportional or regressive over another, so that they cannot always be neatly placed into one category.

Trends in income distribution

The extent to which one would want taxes to be progressive will depend on the scale of pre-tax inequality. If pre-tax incomes were evenly distributed, the tax system would not have much of a role. By contrast, where pre-tax incomes are unequally distributed, the tax system could be a key weapon for those who want to see a fairer distribution of living standards (but by no means the only one). The rest of this section therefore examines what Britain's income distribution actually looks like (Section 15 discusses the distribution of wealth).

Figure 2a shows what has happened to pre-tax incomes (including cash benefits like pensions) since 1949.[1] Until 1978-79, the share of the richest tenth of **families** fell ('families' taken here and elsewhere in this book to mean what is technically called a **tax-unit** – a married couple with or without children or an unmarried individual). Over 30 years, their share fell from a third of all income to just over a quarter (nearly all of this fall affected the top 1%, whose share fell from 11% to 5.3%). In 1978-79, however, the share of the top 10% was still higher than that of the bottom 50%, whose share had risen only slowly and erratically.

Since 1978-79, this has gone into reverse. Unemployment has risen. The gaps between the well paid and the low paid have widened. More of the country's income is paid out as dividends or interest, and less as wages. The value of social security benefits has risen less rapidly than earnings.

Together, these have produced a dramatic shift. The latest figures available are only for the year 1984-85 (as a result of an economy measure which obscures what is happening, they are now produced every three years rather than every year). Nonetheless, in only six years the top 10% had recovered the ground lost in the previous twenty. Meanwhile, the bottom 50% had seen their share fall to its lowest point since the Second World War.

FIGURE 2a

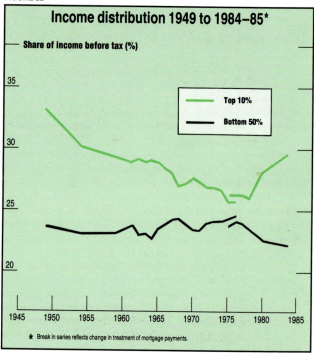

The effects of taxation on the distribution of income

This is the position after allowing for cash benefits but *before* allowing for taxation. What has happened to income *after* all taxes can be seen for more recent years from a different Government source (based on the annual Family Expenditure Survey).[2] Figure 2b compares the situation in 1985 with that in 1979. It shows the distribution between *households,* an important difference from the family unit in Figure 2a (for instance, elderly people living with their children would count as a separate family in Figure 2a – and in most of the analysis in this book – but are included within a larger household in Figure 2b).

Two income bases are shown: **original income** and **income after all taxes and cash benefits.** The first includes pre-tax wages and investment income but excludes pensions and other benefits. The second takes account of benefits and of both direct and indirect taxes. Benefits are the most important reason for the difference between the two bases, greatly increasing the share of those on the lowest incomes. Taken together, direct and indirect taxes have an almost neutral effect on the shares of different income groups. As Section 1 showed, indirect taxes are crucial for those with low incomes: figures for net income only taking account of *direct* taxes ('disposable income') miss the changing balance of taxation.

The different sections of the columns in Figure 2b show the shares received by **quintile groups,** that is, successive fifths of all households arranged by income. If income was completely equally distributed, each group would receive 20% and each column would be divided into five equal parts. This is, of course, far from the case. The bottom quintile group receives virtually no 'original' income: its share fell from 0.5% to 0.3% between 1979 and 1985. By contrast, the richest 20% of households received 45% of original income in 1979, which increased to 49% by 1985.

Taxes and (especially) benefits do reduce this inequality, but to a declining extent. The share of the top 20%, after allowing for benefits and all taxes, was reduced to 40% in 1979, but only to 43% in 1985. Meanwhile, the poorest 20% saw their share fall by a tenth, from 6.1% to 5.6%.

In cash terms, overall household income, after all taxes, rose by 75% over the period. However, most of this was caused by inflation. Working out the change in *real* incomes after all taxes is a little difficult: the usual price indices like the Retail Price Index (RPI) include the effects of indirect tax changes; using the RPI to adjust for inflation would 'double count' them. An index which does not do this is the 'deflator for Gross Domestic Product at factor cost'. This increased by 64% over the period, suggesting that real incomes after all taxes and benefits grew by 7%.

Given that the *share* of the total for the poorest 20% fell from 6.1% to 5.6%, this suggests that their real income, after allowing for all taxes and cash benefits, *fell* by 2% between 1979 and 1985: despite economic growth, the poorest were worse off in *absolute* as well as relative terms.[3] By contrast, the rise in the share of the top 20% meant that they were 15% better off. However, these results should be treated with some caution; not only is the adjustment for inflation difficult, but household composition has changed (one is not quite comparing like with like).

FIGURE 2b

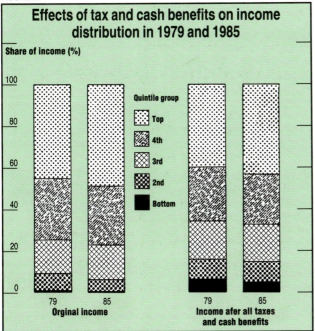

Who are the rich?

The rich, as Hemingway said, *are* different: 'They have more money than we do'.[4] There is a temptation to conclude that income is so unequally distributed that redistribution could be accomplished simply by commandeering the fortunes of a handful of the super-rich like the Duke of Westminster. If this were true, the interests of the middle classes could be preserved while transferring substantial resources to the poor. Only those with earnings many times the 'average' would have to lose out.

Figure 2c suggests a problem with such an approach. It shows the distribution of earnings of all adults in April 1987.[5] 'Average' earnings are often taken as the *mean*

earnings of adult *men* working full-time (indeed, this is the figure used by the Government in producing statistics like those shown in Figures 1a and 1b). In April 1987 this was £224 per week (just under £11,700 in a year).[6] This does not, however, represent a 'typical' earnings figure because this kind of average – total earnings divided by the number of earners – is dragged up by those with very high salaries. Sixty-one per cent of men earn less than the 'average'. Furthermore, women are paid much less than men: only 11% of women working full-time earn more than the male 'average'. Looking at *all* full-time adult employees, 70% earn less than the conventional figure for 'average earnings'. Those working part-time or without employment income at all generally have lower incomes.

FIGURE 2c

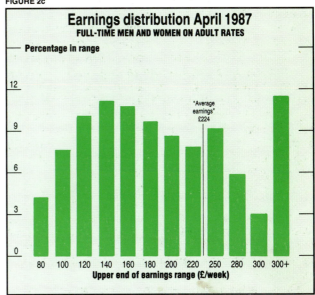

This has important implications. Someone earning 'one and a half times average earnings' does not sound very privileged, and yet they are within the top 10% of the earnings distribution. Someone on 'twice average earnings' (a salary of just over £25,000 in 1988-89) is within the *top 3%* of the earnings distribution. The perceptions of those commenting on tax policy are often coloured by effects on 'ordinary' people like themselves. Journalists on national newspapers and MPs do *not* have ordinary incomes. The box on page 10 explains how the impact of taxation will be described in this book in a way that gives a more accurate impression.

Where is the money?

A further problem is that the way a tax like Income Tax works is that the first slice of income is tax-free, the next is taxed at one rate and the top slice may be taxed at a higher rate (see Sections 5 and 6). When looking at what could be raised by increasing the higher Income Tax rates, it has to be remembered that the bottom part of even the highest income will be below the threshold where the higher rates start; this part will not be affected by the higher rates.

What is the most which could be raised by concentrating on only the highest incomes? The table overleaf shows the total amount of income not already taken in tax ('after tax income') to be found in the slices of taxpayers' incomes *in excess* of certain amounts. These amounts are given in terms of *taxable* income (that is, income after deducting the personal and other allowances described in Section 6). In other words, the table shows what could theoretically be raised if the top Income Tax rate was raised from 40% to 100% above each threshold.

After tax income above various levels[7]

Threshold of taxable income (£/YEAR)	Percentage of taxpayers with incomes above limit	Percentage of all families with incomes above limit	After tax income in excess of limit (£ BILLION)
£40,000	0.9	0.6	3.5
£30,000	1.7	1.2	4.9
£25,000	2.5	1.6	6.2
£20,000	4.5	3.0	8.2
£18,000	6.2	4.1	9.5
£16,000	8.6	5.8	11.4

Obviously, imposing a 100% tax rate on incomes above a certain level would not actually be possible without affecting behaviour. In reality, the amount raised by such a tax would be nothing like that shown – it might be nothing at all. Suppose that *half* of the after tax income above each threshold could be raised in increased tax (which is still dubious – it would mean raising the top tax rate to 70% without provoking changes in behaviour). Then to raise, say, £4 billion would mean putting up taxes on those with taxable incomes of £20,000 and above (as they have a total of £8.2 billion of income above that amount).

This would only affect the top 5% of taxpaying families (the top 3% of all families including non-taxpayers). The bulk of the revenue would come from those with very large incomes indeed, but a small part of it would come from those with incomes of 'only' £25,000 (allowing for the effect of tax allowances) and thus at 'only twice average earnings'. Unless people in such income ranges sustain *some* losses, the scope for raising significant revenue from those on higher incomes is much smaller, as can be worked out from the table.

Showing the effects of tax changes

The shape of the earnings distribution illustrated in Figure 2c means that it can be misleading to look at the effects of taxes by reference, say, to those with 'average' earnings and 5 and 10 times this amount; such earnings levels are not really representative. Such calculations can also be misleading in the assumptions they make about the family structure of the examples. Often, a 'typical' family is used, such as one with a man earning 'average' earnings, a woman without earnings and two children. Such a family is anything but typical. Even allowing for all earnings levels, such families only represent 7% of the total. A widow living alone is, in fact, more 'typical'.[8]

To avoid this type of problem, many of the reforms described below will be examined using a representative sample of all families (to be precise, 5,824 families drawn from the Government's *Family Expenditure Survey*). The effects are shown for successive tenths – **decile groups** – of the income distribution.

A further problem is that a single person with a given income is clearly better off than a couple with two children and the same income. To allow for this, families are arranged in order of their net (after income tax and NICs) **'equivalent' income.** This means dividing a family's income by a certain amount to give the income for a single person who would be placed at the same point in the income distribution.

Exactly how to make this calculation is controversial: how do the costs of living for a couple living together compare with those of two single adults? What allowance should be made for children? The way it is done here is simply to give a weight of 1 for a single person, 1.6 for a couple and 0.4 for each child. Thus a single person with a net income of £10,000 would be placed at the same point in the income distribution as a couple with a joint income of £16,000 and a family of four with a net income of £24,000. This is roughly in line with the way the Government sets Income Support rates. This is *not* to argue that such relativities in fact represent the correct level: it is simply a convenient way of working out roughly where to allocate different families in the distribution. It does not affect the sizes of the gains and losses or the revenue implications of any tax change, just the income group into which different families are allocated.

Figure 2d shows the net equivalent income levels of those placed halfway up each of the successive tenths or decile groups (the 'median' of each group). Thus, a single person with a net income of £240 per week would be in the top decile group. A family of four with the same net income and thus an 'equivalent' income of only £100 per week would be in the sixth decile group. The table shows where particular families would be placed in the distribution.

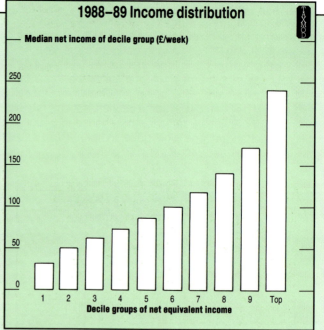

1988–89 Income distribution

Median net income of decile group (£/week)

Decile groups of net equivalent income

FIGURE 2d

The figure is also a powerful reminder of the glaring inequality in living standards left even after taxes and benefits. Those in the top 10% have on average net incomes which are eight times those of the bottom 10%.

Examples of families in each decile group

Decile group	Family type	Net equivalent weekly income
Bottom	Single person (under 25) on Income Support	£41
2nd	Pensioner couple on Income Support	£49
3rd	Single pensioner with £15 per week occupational pension	£62
4th	One earner married couple with 2 children earning £11,000 per year	£72
5th	Single person earning £5,700 per year	£85
6th	One earner married couple with 2 children earning £16,000 per year	£100
7th	Single person earning £8,200 per year	£118
8th	Two earner married couple with 2 children both earning £12,000 per year	£146
9th	Single person earning £12,000 per year	£171
Top	Two earner couple with 2 children both earning £20,000 per year; *or*	£233
	Single person earning £18,700 per year	£255

3. What has happened to the tax system since 1979?

The present government has talked consistently about the need to reduce the level of taxation. What has actually happened is shown in Figure 3a.[1] Far from being lower than it was before 1979, the overall tax ratio (all taxes as a percentage of national income) is *higher* than it was. The gentle decline of the Lawson years has made hardly a dent on the steep rises brought about by the Howe Budgets. The projected effect of the 1988 Budget was, for instance, an insignificant fall from 38% of national income in 1987-88 to 37.9% in 1988-89.

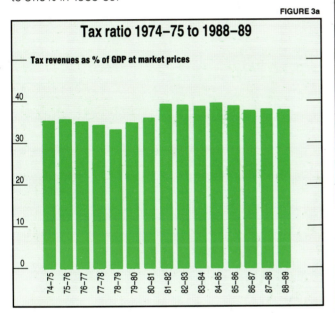

FIGURE 3a

Tax ratio 1974–75 to 1988–89
Tax revenues as % of GDP at market prices

Despite this reality, the popular impression is that taxes *have* been significantly cut. This illusion has been achieved partly through the effect of fading memories – the 1979-1982 period now seems a long time ago. The process of 'fiscal drag' (see box on page 12) also allows governments to claim that they are making tax reductions when in fact they are simply standing still. In addition, there has been a steady shift away from the most highly visible tax, Income Tax, towards those which are less visible (like VAT) or can at least be blamed on someone else (like rates). In 1978-79, Income Tax raised 32% of all tax revenue; by 1988-89, this had fallen to 24% – that is, from almost a third to under a quarter.[2]

This process has happened piece by piece, but each stage has moved gradually in the same direction – the tilt away from a tax structure in which people on higher incomes pay a greater proportion of their income in tax than those on lower incomes. The Poll Tax – under which everyone (except for the limited number receiving rebates) pays the same cash amount, representing the greatest proportion of income for the poor – is simply a logical extension of the process.

Income Tax

It is in the rates of Income Tax that the Government has made the most dramatic changes. The **basic rate** affecting most taxpayers has been cut from 33% to 25% (a rate which applied only to a narrow 'reduced rate band' of income in 1978-79), and the rate applied to the top slice of the highest salaries from 83% to 40% (see Section 5 for a description of how the rate structure works).

At the same time, the **Investment Income Surcharge** which used to be applied to those with significant amounts of investment income (at rates of up to 15% on top of normal Income Tax) has been abolished. This means that, taking account of NICs, investment income is now taxed more lightly than earnings (see Section 12 for some complications, however).

The other important feature of the Income Tax system for most people is the level of the **personal allowances** (see Section 6). Here the pattern has been erratic. In some years such allowances have been increased more rapidly than inflation; in others at the minimum necessary to keep up with it ('statutory indexation'). In 1981 they were not increased at all. Overall, between 1978-79 and 1988-89, the cash value of the single allowance rose by 164% (and the married allowance by 166%) while national income (Gross Domestic Product at market prices) is projected by the Government to have risen by 164%.[3] This means that the allowances have simply risen by the amount needed to avoid increasing the tax burden through fiscal drag.

In 1979, the process of phasing out the old structure of **Child Tax Allowances** (and family allowances) into **Child Benefit,** which has the same value for all children (and is not taxable) was completed. The amount of Income Tax people pay no longer depends on the number of children they have. Before 1977 those with children paid less Income Tax than those with the same income but without children, in recognition of their lower 'taxable capacity'. Instead, *all* those with children now receive Child Benefit. As in part a substitute for Child Tax Allowances, Child Benefit has a dual role as part of both benefit and tax systems.

A further major change will come in 1990-91, when married women will be taxed independently from their husbands (although married men will in most cases retain their more generous tax allowance). Section 8 discusses the distributional effects of this change and Section 9 considers the alternatives.

The Income Tax system is beset with a large range of special allowances and deductions, ostensibly intended to promote objectives like a higher savings rate, which are usually of greatest benefit to those with the highest incomes and flashiest accountants (see Sections 6 and 12). Little has been done to restrict these allowances, the effect of which is to increase the tax *rates* which have to be charged to raise the same revenue from a narrowed tax *base*. Some concessions have been withdrawn, but, in contrast to the 'base broadening' which has accompanied lower tax rates in other countries, new concessions have been introduced – the **Business Expansion Scheme, Personal Equity Plans, Enterprise Zones** and concessions for **share options.** Together these can be used to reduce tax on even the highest incomes to minimal levels. Theoretically, someone with an income of a million pounds could use such devices to avoid tax altogether.[4]

National Insurance Contributions (NICs)

Meanwhile employee NICs – which affect those with earnings, but not with investment income – have been increased, the main rate rising from 6.5% in 1978-79 to 9% from 1983-84 onwards. Those with earnings below £105 per week do now benefit from reduced contribution rates, but nothing has been done to remove the regressive effect of the upper limit on employee contributions (see Section 7).

The Government has raised the 10% employer contribution rate it inherited to 10.45% (with reduced rates where pay is below £155 per week), but has abolished the **National Insurance Surcharge,** which used to be levied on top of these contributions (at a rate which reached a maximum of 3.5% between October 1978 and March 1983). Interestingly, there was remarkably little notice taken when, in 1985, the upper limit was removed for employer contributions so that they now apply to all of the earnings of those on high salaries.

Capital Gains Tax

Those receiving capital gains have also benefited from a steady series of concessions reducing their tax liability: the amount of gain allowed tax-free each year has risen from £1,000 in 1978-79 to £5,000 in 1988-89 and has been extended to become an allowance for all rather than an exemption only for those with small gains; gains which simply reflect inflation are no longer taxed; and gains which took place before 1982 are no longer taxed at all. An important change in the other direction has been that the flat tax rate of 30% was replaced from 1988-89 with the individual's top Income Tax rate, 25% or 40%.

Inheritance Tax

What was once Estate Duty and then Capital Transfer Tax has also been whittled away. Not only has the threshold at which tax becomes payable been increased much faster than prices (from £25,000 to £110,000), but the rates have also been changed from a structure rising from 10% to 75% to one with a single rate of 40%; the tax collected on the largest fortunes has fallen most as a result. The exemption of gifts made more than 7 years before death will now ensure that many inheritances will avoid this tax altogether.

Value Added Tax

One of the Government's first acts in 1979 was to raise the rate of VAT from 8% (on most items) and 12.5% (on 'luxuries') to a single rate of 15%. Apart from this, there have been nibbles at untaxed items, with building repairs and take-away food brought into the VAT net, but there has not yet been a major assault on the 'zero rating' of major areas like food and rent (see Section 16).

Local Authority Rates

Between 1978-79 and 1988-89, the amount raised by local authority rates rose by 216% in cash terms,[5] an increase 20% faster than that of national income. The cause of this increase was not, however, higher spending. Total local authority spending rose by only 138% over the period,[6] a *fall* of 10% relative to national income. What has happened is that the proportion of local government spending met by central government has been cut. In 1978-79, central government grants paid for 61% of 'relevant' local authority spending in England and Wales; the forecast for 1988-89 is 47%.[7] This has meant that central government taxes are lower than they would otherwise have been, with the burden shifted to the rates.

Excise Duties

Because many of the other indirect taxes are expressed as specific cash amounts, they lose their value unless they are uprated to keep up with inflation. Over the last 10 years, the taxes on some items – beer, cigarettes, petrol – have increased more than inflation, while those on others – spirits and wine – have fallen behind inflation (see Section 17). The reasons for these shifts have included 'harmonisation' of duties with the rest of the European Community and health campaigns against tobacco. The net effect has, however, been another shift from the commodities mostly bought by the better off towards those mostly bought by the poor.

Corporation Tax

Ten years ago Corporation Tax was at a rate of 52% on company profits after deducting 100% of the investment made by companies and an allowance for 'stock appreciation' resulting from inflation (see Section 19). In 1984 the rate of tax was cut, and is now 35%, but these allowances were abolished. Since then, revenues have increased. Whereas in 1978-79, Corporation Tax (including a small amount from North Sea revenues) raised less than 7% of all tax revenue, in 1988-89 it will raise nearly 11%.[8]

North Sea Revenues

The last decade has seen revenues from North Sea oil and gas come and largely go. They rose from £0.56 billion in 1978-79 to a peak of £12 billion in 1984-85 but are down to £3.3 billion in 1988-89.[9] In all, some £80 billion of tax revenue will have been collected from the North Sea between 1979-80 and 1988-89 (at 1988-89 prices); a windfall we are unlikely to see again.

Fiscal Drag

If income tax allowances are left unchanged in cash terms as incomes rise, the tax burden (tax as a percentage of income) will rise. This *fiscal drag* occurs because the allowances then represent a smaller proportion of income and a greater proportion is therefore subject to tax. A similar effect occurs if the widths of the bands of the structure of tax rates are not increased: a greater proportion of income becomes liable to tax at the higher rates.

The 'Rooker-Wise-Lawson' amendment to the 1977 Finance Act requires that the main personal income tax allowances have to be increased at least in line with *prices* (unless a specific decision not to do so is announced by the government of the day). However, this kind of indexation only *partly* removes fiscal drag, if, at the time, incomes are rising more rapidly than prices. In order to remove the effects of fiscal drag altogether, allowances would have to be increased by the rate of *income* growth. Other things being equal, the tax burden would then stay unchanged.

Fiscal drag is, however, a gradual and somewhat invisible process. The compensating effect of raising tax allowances has an immediate and visible effect from one pay packet to the next. It is therefore very easy for Chancellors to take credit for 'tax cuts' which are simply the adjustments needed to keep the tax burden constant. The Rooker-Wise-Lawson provisions have had some effect in reducing the extent to which this works, but governments continue to get the credit for any increase in allowances in excess of prices, even though allowances have increased by no more than has been needed to keep up with incomes.

The combined effect of tax and benefit changes since 1979

The benefit system has also changed in the last 10 years. Some benefits like Housing Benefit have been explicitly cut; others, like pensions, have been allowed to lag behind national income growth so that recipients have been cut off from much of the rise in national prosperity.

Although this book is not primarily about benefits, it is instructive to look at benefits and tax changes together. Specifically, Figures 3b, 3c and 3d compare the 1978-79 and 1988-89 structures of benefits and *direct* taxes (Income Tax and employee National Insurance Contributions). The figures show the differences between taxes and benefits under the actual 1988-89 system and those which would have resulted from the 1978-79 system *if it had been uprated in line with national income growth* (that is, by 164%).[10] For taxes, this eliminates the effects of fiscal drag; for benefits, it amounts to saying that the 'neutral' position would have been one in which benefits stayed in line with national income, which seems the fairest starting point.

The '1978-79' system therefore includes Income Tax rates of up to 83%, allowances increased by 164% from their actual 1978-79 levels, Investment Income Surcharge, National Insurance Contributions at 6.5% and so on. The benefit rates are a weighted average of those paid during 1978-79 (they changed in November 1978) increased by 164%. This would, for instance, mean a single pension of £48.18 (compared with the actual 1988-89 level of £41.15). The comparison also includes the effects of the change to Income Support, Family Credit and the new system of Housing Benefit from the old system of Supplementary Benefit, Family Income Supplement (FIS) and rent and rate rebates. *Indirect* taxes are *not* taken into account.

Remarkably, what has happened has been a virtually zero net cost reform: *the cuts in direct taxes have been entirely paid for by cuts in the generosity of benefits*. In 1988-89, Income Tax and employee NICs will raise approximately £20 billion more than the benefits covered by the calculations; under the adjusted '1978-79' system, the difference would have been only £0.2 billion less.

There has, however, been a major redistribution from those on low incomes to the better off. Figure 3b shows the net effects on the 'decile groups' described in Section 2.

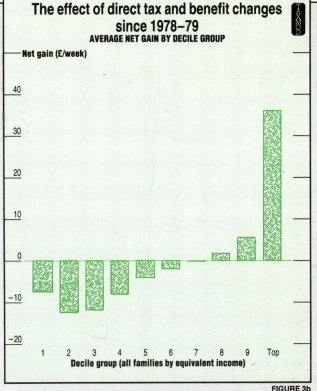

FIGURE 3b

Overall, the bottom 60% of the income distribution has lost, while the top 30% – especially the top 10% – has gained (relative to the starting point of the adjusted '1978-79' system). The losses for the bottom 50% average out at nearly £8.50 per family – a substantial proportion of the net incomes shown in Figure 2d – while the top 10% have gained nearly £40 per family. Overall, the bottom half of the population has lost £6.6 billion, of which £5.6 billion has gone to the top 10%; indeed, £4.8 billion has gone to the top 5%.

Figures 3c and 3d show the proportions of the families in each group gaining and losing. Overall, 57% of families have lost and 40% have gained. Within this, the overwhelming majority of the bottom half of the distribution have lost; the overwhelming majority of the top 30% have gained. Section 20 discusses a package of measures which would reverse this shift.

FIGURE 3c

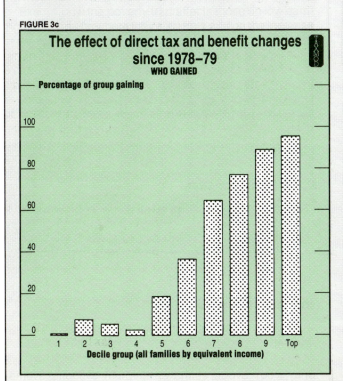

FIGURE 3d

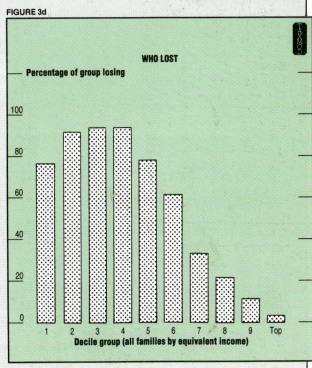

4. An international comparison

The tax systems of other countries are of interest for two reasons. First, their solutions to similar problems may suggest what could be possible here. For instance, the argument that a local income tax would be 'administratively impossible' is hard to sustain when Belgium, Canada, Denmark, Finland, Norway, Sweden and the USA already have one.

Secondly, within an increasingly integrated world economy the tax systems of other countries constrain our own. If one country charges a much higher rate of tax on company profits than others, multinational corporations will try to ensure that their profits arise in the country with the lowest tax rate by manipulating the prices at which inputs and components are sold between their own divisions in different countries ('transfer pricing'). Individual countries can do a little to limit this kind of activity and it may not be worthwhile if the rate differentials are small; but large differentials will be hard to maintain.

Overall tax burden

Britain is not a high tax country. Figure 4a shows the proportion of national income which all taxes and social security contributions represent in nineteen Western countries belonging to the Organisation for Economic Co-operation and Development (OECD).[1] The ratio shown is with Gross National Product (GNP) at 'factor cost', that is, at

prices *excluding* indirect taxes and subsidies. This avoids a misleading comparison between countries relying on indirect taxes to varying degrees. It gives a somewhat higher ratio than to Gross Domestic Product (GDP) at market prices as shown in Figure 3a.

Britain is in the middle of the distribution, with higher overall taxes than countries like Japan or the USA but lower ones than most of the rest of Western Europe. The figure shows no obvious link between tax ratios and growth rates: low-tax Japan and high-tax Norway are the countries which have had the best growth performances over the last fifteen years.

Nor was the rise in the British tax burden between 1975 and 1985, from 40% to 45% (of GNP at factor cost) unusual. While the tax ratio did not rise very much in West Germany or the USA, the rise was 7 percentage points in Japan, 10 in France and 14 in Italy.[2]

Tax structure

Where Figure 4a does show that Britain is slightly unusual is in the ratio of *indirect* taxes to GNP, particularly given its overall tax ratio. Apart from the four highest tax countries, only Austria and Greece raise so much revenue from indirect taxes in relation to national income. A more detailed comparison for the six large economies is shown in Figure 4b.[3] Britain is the only one where indirect taxes account for more than 40% of tax revenues. Conversely, only in France is a lower share raised from direct taxes on individuals plus employee social security contributions (Income Tax and NICs in Britain). All the other countries raise a higher proportion of their revenue from employer social security contributions, particularly France.

FIGURE 4a

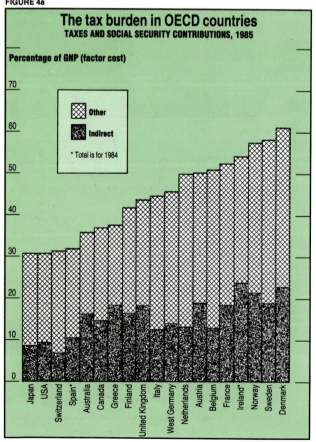

FIGURE 4b

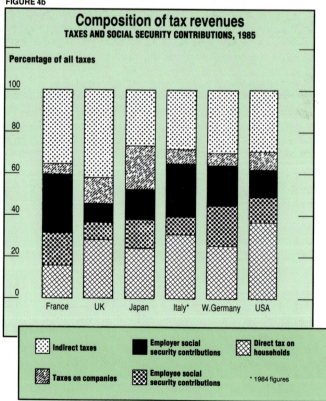

Income Tax rates

In comparing different countries' tax systems, almost as much depends on *what* is taxed – the **tax base** – as on the *rate* at which it is taxed. Differences in tax allowances, the scope of what is taxable and in the tax treatment of marriage (see Section 9) have an important bearing on how the systems work. Analysing these would, however, take more space than is available here, so the table below presents information on the more limited subject of income tax rates. The table shows individual income tax structures for the same nineteen countries as Figure 4a, with the countries ranked in order of the highest marginal tax rate (see Section 5) on those with high incomes, including local taxes and employee social security contributions where appropriate.

Direct individual tax structures, 1988

| | National income tax | | | Maximum marginal tax rate (%) including local income tax and employee social security contributions[1] |
	Bottom rate %	Top rate %	Number of bands	
Belgium	24	71.2	13	81
Japan	10.5	60	12	76 (65 proposed)
Sweden	5	45	4	75
Finland	38	51	4	72.5 (65.5 proposed)
Netherlands	14	72	9	72 (60 planned)
Denmark	22	40	3	68
Spain	32	56	11	65.2
Norway	10	29	4	63.2
Italy	12	62	9	62 (60 planned)
Austria	39	62	5	62 (50 planned)
Ireland	35	58	3	59
France	5	56.8	12	62.4
West Germany	22	56	★	56 (53 proposed)
Australia	24	49	4	50.25
Greece	18	50	9	50
USA	15	33	3	46
Canada	17	29	3	44.81
United Kingdom	25	40	2	40
Switzerland	1	13	7	26.2

1. Applying to those with *high* incomes; withdrawal of social security benefits not taken into account.
★ Income tax rate structure in West Germany is a curve rather than a series of bands.
SOURCES: *Individual Taxes: A Worldwide Summary*, 1988 edition, London: Price Waterhouse World Firm Limited; *World Tax Reform: A Progress Report*, J.A. Pechman (ed), Washington DC: Brookings Institution, 1988; National sources and press reports.

Three things stand out:

■ Despite Britain's middling overall tax ratio, the top income tax rate (now 40%) is one of the lowest. If one includes the effects of local income taxes (very important in Norway and Sweden) and social security contributions (where, unlike in Britain, these affect the top slices of high incomes), our top rate of 40% is lower than anywhere else except low tax Switzerland;

■ Britain's *starting* rate of national income tax – 25% – is only exceeded in four of the countries;

■ All of the other countries have more than two bands in their income tax structure, most of them having several (see Section 5 for a discussion of the merits of such 'graduated' tax structures).

There has been a clear trend towards lower top tax rates (with several more reductions to come, as shown), but it has been carried further in Britain than anywhere else. It should also be remembered that, unlike in Britain, elsewhere when top rates have been cut (such as the USA or Australia), other 'base broadening' measures have been introduced at the same time which have offset the cuts in tax rates.[4]

Company Tax rates

There has also been an international trend towards lower company tax rates. Much of the reason for this stems from disillusionment with previous strategies involving higher tax rates, but generous tax-free allowances for favoured activities like investment. Cuts in tax rates have therefore been accompanied by 'base-broadening' reductions in allowances, so that revenues from company taxes have risen rather than fallen. The 1984 Corporation Tax reform in Britain (see Section 19) was in line with this (indeed, it set the pattern for several other countries; others like Sweden are likely to follow). As the table below shows, the British company tax rate is now one of the lowest in the OECD area.

For the reason mentioned at the start of the section, it is hard for one country to keep a high company tax rate when rates in other countries are much lower. The recent rate reductions in several countries have also therefore had something of the character of an auction to attract profits to whatever emerges as the best 'tax haven'. As national governments undercut one another, it will be the owners of multinationals who benefit.

Company Tax rates, 1988

(Percentage rate charged on undistributed profits)

West Germany	56 (50 planned)
Sweden	52
Japan	52
Denmark	50
Finland	49 (44 planned; includes 16 local tax)
Greece	49
Italy	46
Canada	43.5 (includes 15.5 provincial)
Belgium	43
France	42
Australia	39
USA	39
Netherlands	35
Spain	35
United Kingdom	35

SOURCES: *World Tax Reform: A Progress Report*, J.A. Pechman (ed), Washington DC: Brookings Institution, 1988; *Comparative Tax Systems: Europe, Canada and Japan*, J.A. Pechman (ed), Arlington: Tax Analysts, 1987; National sources and press reports.

Rates of Value Added Tax (VAT) elsewhere in Europe

Finally, particularly in the light of the European Commission's proposals for VAT harmonisation (see Section 16), it is interesting to compare Britain's VAT structure with that of other Community members. As can be seen from the table, only Denmark has a structure like Britain's with just one rate of tax. Most of the countries have reduced rates on items which in Britain would be zero-rated; only Ireland and Portugal also apply a zero rate to a wide range of items. Half of the countries have a higher rate of VAT on certain 'luxuries'. Britain's standard rate of 15% is lower than that in most of the other countries.

VAT rates in the European Community, April 1987

	Standard rate	Higher rate(s)	Reduced rate(s)	Scope of zero rate
Belgium	19	25,33	6, 17	Newspapers
Denmark	22	—	—	Newspapers, large ships and aircraft
France	18.6	33.3	5.5,7	—
Germany	14	—	7	—
Greece	18	36	6	—
Ireland	25	—	10	Wide range
Italy	18	38	2, 9	Newspapers
Luxembourg	12	—	3, 6	—
Netherlands	20	—	6	—
Portugal	16	30	8	Basic foods, medicines and newspapers
Spain	12	33	6	—
United Kingdom	15	—	—	Wide range

SOURCE: Reproduced from *Fiscal Harmonisation: An Analysis of the European Commission's Proposals* by Catherine Lee, Mark Pearson and Stephen Smith (IFS Report Series No.28, 1988, London: IFS).

5. The structure of income tax rates

The Income Tax system is structured so that not only do those on higher incomes pay more tax than those on lower ones, but they also pay a greater *proportion* of income in tax. So long as this proportion – the **average rate** of tax on someone's whole income – rises as income rises, the tax system will be progressive and reduce inequality (see Section 2).

The first way this progressivity is achieved is through the tax-free **personal allowance** which everyone receives. The majority of taxpayers pay tax at the **basic rate** of 25% on the **taxable income** left after deducting the personal allowance (and any other allowances) from total income.

For a single person the allowance for 1988-89 is £2,605. Thus a single person with an annual income of £5,000 pays £598.75 in tax (25% of £2,395). On an income of £10,000, tax is £1,848.75 (25% of £7,395). Although these two taxpayers both face the same rate of tax – 25% – on any additional income they receive (their **marginal rate** of tax is the same), the system is progressive. The first person pays 12.0% of their total income in tax, the second 18.5%. This is because the tax-free personal allowance is a greater share of the lower income than of the higher one.

Figure 5a shows how average rates of tax rise with income, even within the basic rate band. It also shows the limitations of relying on allowances and a single tax rate to achieve progressivity. At first average tax rates rise quite steeply, but after a while they level out: only 21.7% of an income of £20,000 would be paid in tax, a proportion only just above that paid by someone with half as much income.

It is only for incomes above this that the **higher rate** takes effect. While the first £19,300 of someone's taxable income is taxed at the basic rate of 25%, income above this is taxed at 40%. Thus, someone with an income of £30,000 pays £8,063 in tax (with £2,605 tax-free, £19,300 taxed at 25% and £8,095 taxed at 40%).

As can be seen from the figure, the onset of the 40% rate does mean that the average rate begins to rise more sharply, but then it levels out again. In any case, only a very small minority of taxpayers are affected by the higher rate: 94% of taxpayers pay at the basic rate.

Until 1988, successive slices of the highest incomes were taxed at increasing rates – 45%, 50%, 55% and 60%. This did not mean, of course, that *all* of someone's income was taxed at, say, 45%, just the top slices. Abolition of the top rates has been a major part of the redistribution towards the rich illustrated in Figure 3b.

The wide basic rate band

The UK system is unusual in Europe in having a wide band of income subject to a single rate. In most other countries income tax generally starts at a lower rate and the bands subject to each rate of tax are narrower. Having such a wide basic rate band does have some advantages:

■ Collecting tax at source (from banks, building societies, etc) on non-employment income like dividends and interest is much easier when virtually all taxpayers are taxed at the same rate. Combined with the PAYE system for employment income, this means that the Inland Revenue can avoid direct contact with most individual taxpayers.

■ Taxation of husband and wife presents a number of problems (see Sections 8 and 9), some of which – in particular, taxing investment income – are easier if both partners face the same tax rate.

■ The system is easy to understand, perhaps misleadingly so. The Government has been able to give the impression that it has cut taxes, when the basic rate has been virtually the *only* element of the tax system as a whole affecting most people which has been cut.

The problem has been described above: the wide basic rate band means that for many income levels, Income Tax is hardly at all progressive (as Section 7 shows, the situation is even worse when one adds in the peculiar structure of NICs). But if the wide basic rate was abandoned, some way would be needed to get round the administrative problems which would result from coping with several marginal rates (a problem which other countries have solved, but at the cost of more people having to complete tax returns).

Increases in the higher rates

The box discusses the arguments as to whether there are economic limits to the level of tax rates. Notwithstanding these arguments, the revenue potential of higher rates above their current starting point is limited by the numbers who pay them – only 5%-6% of taxpayers. Restoring the 45%-60% bands which were abolished in the 1988 Budget would raise about £1,700 million (with the bands based on those applying in 1987-88 but indexed for inflation and with the starting point for the 40% band at its present £19,300).[1]

As Section 2 shows, very large amounts of revenue cannot be gathered by concentrating only on the highest slices of incomes. Having restored the old higher rates, increasing the top rate from 60% to 70% (on taxable income above £43,500) would raise only a further £500 million. What is at least as important is the *starting point* for the higher rates – lowering this would increase the proportion of taxpayers paying at the higher rates. For instance, reducing the starting point for the restored higher rate bands from £19,300 of taxable income to £16,400 would

FIGURE 5a

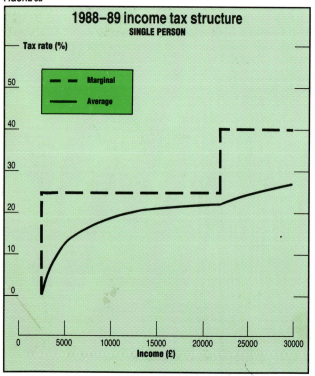

1988–89 income tax structure
SINGLE PERSON

Limits to tax rates

The main limits to tax rates are political. Unless the political case for redistribution is won, the discussion here is of little relevance. There are, however, genuine arguments about the economic effects of taxation which should not be ignored. If they are, redistribution can be presented as economically damaging and easily dismissed.

The main accusation is that high taxes on the rich act as a 'disincentive' and reduce economic growth, eventually lowering everyone's living standards. Despite the frequency with which such a claim is made, there seems to be little evidence to support it, despite substantial research on both sides of the Atlantic (see the references under 'Where to find out more').

One reason why tax rates seem to have little effect on labour supply is that higher taxes have two effects. On the one hand, if the tax system removes a larger slice of additional income, say from overtime (that is, if there is a high *marginal* tax rate), the amount people are prepared to work may be cut back (this is known as the 'substitution effect'). On the other hand, a heavier tax burden overall (a high *average* tax rate) will make it more difficult to achieve the standard of living people want without working more (the 'income effect'). The balance of these could go either way. Recent UK studies suggest that, for men, lower taxes would on balance *reduce* hours worked by a small amount.[2]

A second reason is that most people are simply not in a position to decide that they would rather work 30 hours than 38 (although they may be able to choose between different careers and to decide when to retire – decisions which may also be affected by taxation). The working week is given, and people have to accept it. For those on the highest incomes, job satisfaction and status are probably more important motivations than cash by itself.

Where research *has* shown sensitivity to taxation, however, is for married women. Many are in the position where they are deciding whether to take a paid job and, if so, how many hours to work, balancing the returns from doing so against childcare costs.

This apart, there are two constraints which really do seem important in setting economic limits to taxation. The first is that people with particular skills may have the option of going abroad if they could improve their standard of living by doing so. Even here, emigration of British doctors and scientists may be more likely to result from under-funding of the NHS and the neglect of research; the problem is one of public spending cuts, not high tax rates.

The second is tax avoidance and evasion.[3] It is very hard to tax some forms of income – such as capital gains and fringe benefits – completely effectively. If individuals' regular income is taxed very heavily, it will be worth their while to engage in the most complicated (and economically wasteful) exercises to transform it into another form. The 98% tax rate, which could in theory apply to the investment income of top taxpayers before 1979, was daft: no one with a decent accountant paid it. Worse than that, it supported a fiction that the tax system was more progressive than it really was, blocking the way for progressive reform and giving ammunition to the case that taxation is economically damaging.

raise an extra £700 million, without any further change in tax *rates*.

A more progressive rate structure

Figure 5b shows how a more even rise in average tax rates than now could be achieved by a **graduated** rate structure. Many variants are possible; the one illustrated combines the restoration of 45% and 50% bands (on taxable income above £19,400 and £24,400 respectively) with breaking the basic rate band in two, replacing it with a 22% rate on the first £8,400 of taxable income (up to near 'average' earnings) and a new 34% band up to a £16,400 starting point for the 40% band.

This structure would raise roughly the same amount as the actual 1988-89 structure (in fact, roughly £70 million more according to TAXMOD). Those with taxable incomes below £11,200 (and hence with income before allowances of at least £13,800) would gain. Overall, 55% of all families would gain, while only 13% would lose (the others are non-taxpayers). Figure 5c shows that the change would be progressive, only the top decile group losing on average. As the majority of people earn less than 'average' earnings, nearly twice as many taxpayers would see a *fall* in their marginal tax rate as an increase – in this sense, it would actually 'improve' incentives.

Section 6 discusses whether increasing allowances while retaining a (higher) wide basic rate band to pay for this would be a better way of changing the rate structure than introducing graduation.

FIGURE 5b

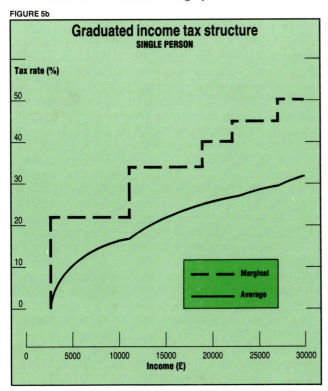

FIGURE 5c

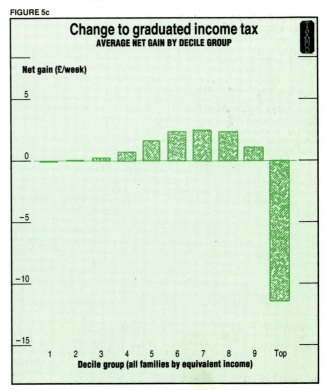

6. Income tax allowances

As well as the single person's allowance there are other allowances, the most important of which are listed in the table (for 1988-89). Thus, for instance, while a single person earning £10,000 would have a taxable income of £7,395, a married man earning the same would only have a taxable income of £5,905, after allowing for the **Married Man's Allowance.** Married women are entitled to the equivalent of the single allowance – the **Wife's Earned Income Allowance** – as an allowance against their *earned* income only. The operation of both of these allowances and the way they will change in 1990 is described in Section 8. Those over 65 can claim the **age allowances** which are somewhat higher than the normal personal allowances.

Other allowances, like tax relief for pension contributions and mortgage interest, also reduce taxable income. In the latter case, the equivalent of the tax reduction is given not through the PAYE system, but through the **Mortgage Interest Relief at Source** (MIRAS) system, under which the borrower makes *net* payments of mortgage interest and the lender claims the relief.

Main personal and other allowances, 1988-89	
Single person	£2,605
Married man	£4,095
Wife's earned income	£2,605
Age allowance – single	£3,180 (£3,310 over 80)
– married	£5,035 (£5,205 over 80)
Employee pension contributions	
Interest on mortgages (up to interest on a loan of £30,000)	

The effects of the allowances

As Section 5 showed, the personal allowances ensure that Income Tax is progressive (albeit to a rather limited extent above average earnings). They also delay the starting point for the higher rate of tax. The 40% band does not start until someone has £19,300 of *taxable* income. This could correspond to total income of anything from £21,905 (someone only receiving the £2,605 single allowance) to over £28,000 (a married man with £3,000 of mortgage interest and making some pension contributions).

Allowances – and increases in them – are thus worth *more* to higher rate taxpayers than to those paying at the basic rate. An extra £100 on a basic ratepayer's allowance reduces tax by £25. But for someone paying tax at 40%, the £100 reduction in taxable income will reduce tax by £40. If higher rates above 40% were restored, the effect would be even larger for those with the highest incomes. Higher rate taxpayers thus receive a greater benefit from their mortgage tax relief than everyone else.

Exemptions instead of allowances?

One way of restricting this effect would be to change allowances into **exemptions,** similar to the Lower Earnings Limit for NICs. Anyone with income below an exemp-

tion pays no tax at all, but those above it cannot deduct anything; all their income is taxed. The objection to such a system is that the resulting structure involves undesirable sudden jumps in tax liability at particular income levels and means that everyone above the exemption pays the same proportion of income in tax, removing progressivity (this is one of the main problems with NICs – see Section 7).

A device suggested to cope with this is the idea of **vanishing exemptions.** These would act like allowances up to a certain income level, above which they would be gradually withdrawn in a way which avoided jumps in tax liability. The age allowances actually works in this way already. If income before allowances exceeds £10,600, the age allowance is gradually reduced to the size of the ordinary personal allowance. The new US tax structure embodies a similar feature. Such devices are, however, really just a rather roundabout way of increasing marginal tax rates. For elderly British taxpayers there is a jump in the tax charged on any additional pound of income from 25% to 42% (higher than the top rate for non-pensioners) as the extra allowance is withdrawn, after which it drops back again to 25%. Similarly, the marginal rates in the new US structure jump from 28% to 33% and then fall back again. If one wants to increase marginal tax rates, there are other (simpler and neater) methods.

Restricting allowances to the basic rate

Another way of reforming allowances which would also increase the revenue from higher rate tax would be to set the allowances against *basic rate* tax only, so that they did not affect liabilities to the higher rates. It is easiest to see how this would work in the case of mortgage interest relief. Relief at the 25% basic rate is already given through MIRAS. The *extra* relief for those who pay tax at the higher rate has to be worked out by the Inland Revenue after someone submits a tax return. A 40% taxpayer is entitled to an extra 15% of tax relief, for instance. Thus, while a basic rate taxpayer with gross monthly interest of £300 receives relief worth £75, a 40% taxpayer gets £120. Restricting the mortgage interest relief to the basic rate would simply involve removing the second stage of the process: MIRAS would be the *only* form of relief, and all borrowers would be treated in the same way.

With the abolition of the tax rates above 40%, such a change would not be as important in terms of revenue-raising as it used to be. Within the 1988-89 structure, the Government estimates that the additional revenue raised from restricting mortgage interest relief to the basic rate would be some £280 million per year.[1] However, if some or all of the higher rates above 40% were restored, and if the starting point for the higher rates was lower than now, the revenue gain could be significant. One could attempt to achieve the same effect for relief on employee pension contributions, but it is likely that the restriction could be easily avoided in this case by means of a switch towards employer pension contributions (a switch which has already occurred in many cases as a way of minimising NICs).

A much more important shift could be achieved if the *personal allowances* were restricted to the basic rate. There are two ways in which this could be done. The first is through a **tax credit** system. Under such a system, instead of deducting an allowance to give the total on which tax is calculated, tax is calculated on the whole of income, but then a fixed amount – the tax credit – is deducted for each taxpayer. Thus, instead of the single allowance of £2,605, there could be a credit of £651.25 (25% of £2,605). Someone on the basic rate would end up paying the same amount as now: for instance, the tax on an income of £10,000 would be £2,500 *less* the credit of £651.25, giving £1,848.75, as now.

Higher rate taxpayers would, however, be affected (especially if some of the higher rates above 40% were restored). Assuming that the starting point of the 40% band was left unchanged at £19,300 (but now applied to income *before* deducting allowances), someone with income of £21,000 would now pay tax at 40% on the top £1,700 slice of income; the allowance would no longer keep them within the basic rate band. Furthermore, an *increase* in the tax credit would have no effect on higher rate tax payable and so would be of the same value to all taxpayers. It is this logic which led, for instance, to the conversion of the Child Tax Allowances which existed before 1979-80 into an equal payment of **Child Benefit.** The previous Child Tax Allowances had been worth most to the highest rate taxpayers.

One drawback of a tax credit system is that it is not immediately obvious where the starting point for paying tax is: £651.25 somehow does not *sound* as valuable as the current single allowance. A presentationally more attractive way of achieving the same effect is that of a **Zero Rate Band.** Under this, one would simply say that instead of the current personal allowance, the first £2,605 of a single person's income would be taxed at a zero rate; income between £2,605 and £19,300 would be taxed at the basic rate; the next slice at 40% and so on. As with a tax credit, any change in the width of the Zero Rate Band would not affect the starting point for higher rate tax and would be worth the same for all taxpayers.

For technical reasons,[2] introducing a Zero Rate Band within the current structure of joint taxation of married couples would be rather complicated. However, within a system of independent taxation of married couples (see Section 9), a Zero Rate Band could have useful effects (and is used in the package described in Section 20).

If allowances were restricted to the basic rate, existing higher rate taxpayers would, of course, pay more tax because they no longer received relief at the higher rates. In addition, some taxpayers who are currently kept below the higher rate threshold by the allowances would be brought above it: the 40% band would start at income equal to £19,300, not at a point some way above it. The substitution of a Zero Rate Band for the current single allowance would thus have a very similar revenue-raising effect to a £2,605 reduction of the starting points for higher rate tax.

Minimum taxes and maximum allowances

Given the great variety of allowances which can be claimed, it is possible for those on even the highest incomes to avoid paying very much – or even any – tax. As mentioned above, someone with an income of a million pounds could theoretically pay no tax at all.[3] While this is unlikely, it is certainly true that those on higher incomes make more use of allowances and deductions than those on low incomes. In 1984-85, the 5% of taxpayers with the highest total incomes claimed deductions (*not* including mortgage interest or personal allowances) equivalent to 4% of their incomes, compared with 0.6% for the bottom half of taxpayers.[4]

One way to restrict this would be to introduce a **minimum tax** of the kind which exists in the USA (and was strengthened in the 1986 US tax reform). Under this, two calculations are made when assessing tax. The first uses the regular tax schedule and allowances in the normal way. The second – only made for those with high incomes – works out tax on a different schedule, but with restricted allowances. The taxpayer has to pay the *higher* of these two amounts. This limits the extent to which allowances can reduce tax bills.

For example, suppose that the minimum tax was 40% of gross income in excess of £25,000 (with no other allowances). Someone with a gross income of £100,000 would thus have to pay a minimum tax of £30,000 no matter how many deductions their accountant came up with. For people claiming only the personal allowances and a few other ones, the regular tax calculation would always be higher, and they would not be affected by the minimum tax.

An alternative way of cutting out excessive use of tax allowances would be to set a cash figure for the **maximum allowance** which anyone could claim. This would have a very similar effect to the minimum tax, but would also have the advantage that if the figure remained the same in *cash* from year to year while the personal allowances rose, it would gradually cut back the other allowances – hence broadening the tax base – without causing any sudden jumps in tax liabilities.

Rate cuts versus allowance increases

Income Tax cuts can be achieved in two main ways – cutting tax rates or increasing the value of allowances. The distributional effects of the two are very different, as Figure 6a shows (the figure does not allow for the effects of tax cuts on means-tested benefits – these reduce the value of either kind of tax cut to those at the bottom of the income distribution – see Section 10). The two changes illustrated – a 2 pence cut in the basic rate and a 14% increase in the main personal allowances – would have the same cost (a revenue reduction of £2.8 billion). Their values at different income levels vary greatly, however.

FIGURE 6a

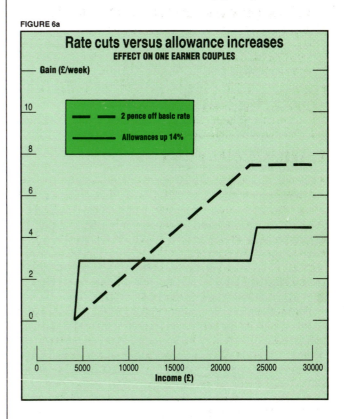

The value of the 2 pence cut in the basic rate depends on the individual's taxable income and is worth most at the top of the basic rate band – £7.42 per week. By contrast, the rise in the value of allowances (in this case of the married man's allowance from £4,095 to £4,670) is worth the same £2.76 per week to all those in the basic rate band

(and a little more to those in the higher rate band for the reasons discussed above). The increase in allowances is clearly a much more progressive way of cutting taxes – if this is the policy objective – than cutting the basic rate.

Allowance increases rather than a graduated rate structure?

Following on from this, it has been suggested[5] that, rather than changing Income Tax to give it a graduated rate structure (as proposed in Section 5) it would be better to concentrate on raising tax *allowances* while retaining the wide basic rate. In order to pay for the higher allowances, the basic rate would have to be higher than now. Figure 6b shows the effects of an example of this kind of change, in which the personal allowances are raised by 12.5% (so that the single allowance rises from £2,605 to £2,930 and the Married Man's Allowance from £4,095 to £4,605), paid for by raising the basic rate from 25% to 27%. This raises about the same revenue as the graduated structure illustrated in Figure 5b (a revenue gain of about £100 million compared with the current system).

FIGURE 6b

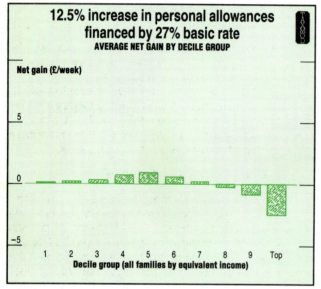

The redistribution involved in this particular change is of a rather smaller scale than that shown in Figure 5c. Relatively speaking, however, the gains shown in Figure 6b *are* more concentrated on those lower down the earnings scale. The largest gain goes to the fifth decile group from the bottom, as opposed to the seventh decile group in Figure 5c. This is because a rise in allowances is worth more to someone right at the bottom of the basic rate band than a cut in the starting rate of tax from 25% to 22%. In this sense, the increase in allowances *is* more progressive than the graduated rate structure.

However, this is only part of the story. First, despite the smaller scale of redistribution involved, the change illustrated in Figure 6b implies losses for 31% of families (as against 13% for the graduated structure) and gains for only 36% (as against 55%). The 'break-even point' at which the 2 pence higher basic rate wipes out the increased allowances is an income of £7,000 for a single person or £11,000 for a married man. These compare with break-even points of £13,800 for a single person or £15,300 for a married man when switching to the graduated structure shown in Figure 5b. Under the allowance increase, the losers start from a lower income level and are therefore much more numerous.

A second problem with the strategy of retaining an (in-

The 'cost' of tax allowances

Allowances reduce the tax revenue Government would otherwise receive. They therefore have a similar – if less visible – effect on public finances to public spending. In recent years the Government has listed the cost of **tax expenditures** in its annual public spending White Paper.[6] Some of these costs are substantial, as can be seen from the list below. However, one has to be careful with such numbers. For instance, the 'cost' of the main personal allowances was £25 billion in 1987-88. But, as we have seen, these allowances are a crucial part of the tax structure, giving it progressivity; it would be a mistake to count this figure in its entirety into a calculation of the cost of tax expenditures. Similarly, the 'cost' of some pension reliefs (not those listed below) could not actually be recouped if the tax system was altered.

Cost of major tax reliefs, 1987-88 (£ million)

Mortgage interest relief	£4,750
Exemption of pension fund income	£4,100
Tax-free lump sums to pensioners	£1,200
Pre-1984 insurance premiums	£ 520
Age allowance	£ 390

creased) wide basic rate band while increasing allowances is that marginal tax rates are higher for virtually all taxpayers except for the few taken out of tax altogether and those paying at the higher rate. Even averaging out over all taxpayers, the change shown in Figure 6b involves a *greater* rise in marginal tax rates than that illustrated in Figures 5b and 5c.

Given that less redistribution is accomplished at a greater cost in terms of both the number of losers and in terms of marginal tax rates (and hence 'incentives'), this alternative to a graduated rate structure does not seem to have much to recommend it, particularly if one is trying to build wide political support for a redistributive package.

At the heart of this there is a more fundamental point. Few would argue that tax policy should be decided simply on the basis of what happens to those right at the bottom. Others, somewhat higher up the income distribution, are important as well. Once one has decided the point at which taxation should start, there is no reason why one should then be constrained to choose a structure of average tax rates which rise in the peculiar way they do now (as illustrated in Figure 5a). And yet, that kind of curve, which first rises steeply and then flattens out, is inherent to a system which incorporates a wide basic rate band. A graduated structure avoids this constraint.

Having said all of which, the narrow 'reduced rate band' which existed until the year 1979-80 did not constitute a 'graduated structure'. In this case, higher personal allowances *would* have been a more effective way of reducing taxes at the bottom of the distribution. The advantages of the kind of structure illustrated in Figure 5b arise because the basic rate band is broken at around average earnings, which is precisely the point where the problem of average tax rates levelling out currently occurs.

7. Employee national insurance contributions

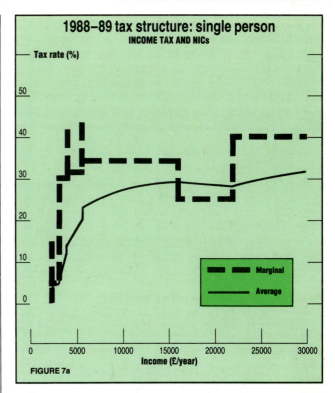

FIGURE 7a

People with earnings pay another tax on top of Income Tax – **National Insurance Contributions,** or 'NICs'. Employers also make contributions on their employees' behalf; these and the contributions made by the self-employed are described in Section 19. This separate tax system was set up as a way of financing – and determining entitlement to – benefits like the state retirement pension and Unemployment Benefit. As the relationship between contributions and benefits is in many cases indistinct, NICs are increasingly seen as a form of direct tax, but one whose structure does not relate very well to that of Income Tax.

For most of those who are not 'contracted out' of the **State Earnings Related Pension Scheme** (SERPS), employee NICs are equal to 9% of earnings *up to* the **Upper Earnings Limit** of £305 per week (1988-89). Those with earnings below the **Lower Earnings Limit** of £41 per week are exempted from making contributions, while those between £41 and £70 pay at 5%, and those between £70 and £105 at 7%. Note that the appropriate rate is applied to *total* earnings in each case. Liability thus jumps from nothing to £2.05 per week as earnings increase over the lower limit and there are similar jumps at £70 and £105. Once earnings are above £105, everyone pays the same percentage of income in tax – it is thus **proportional** rather than progressive until the upper limit is reached. After that, contributions decrease as a proportion of income: over this range they are **regressive.**

Other features of the system include a lower rate of contributions for those **contracted out** of SERPS (because their occupational pension scheme guarantees pensions at a minimum level set by the Government). This rebate currently lowers the contribution rate by 2 percentage points. Certain married women contribute at a lower rate and have reduced entitlement to contributory benefits. The number of women in this position is declining, but there are still approximately one million in 1988-89.[1] There are also special arrangements for the self-employed (see Section 19).

The interaction of NICs and Income Tax

The curious structure resulting from the combination of Income Tax and NICs is illustrated in Figure 7a. Section 5 has already shown the way in which Income Tax has only limited progressivity over the income range above average earnings. If one looks at the total of the two, the picture is even worse as a result of the Upper Earnings Limit. Below the limit the marginal tax rate is 34% (25% plus 9%); above it is a 'dip' where only the basic rate of 25% is payable until the 40% Income Tax rate is reached.

What is important for the progressivity of the tax system is the resultant structure of *average* tax rates. These also fall between the Upper Earnings Limit and the start of the 40% band. This means that people on higher incomes pay a *smaller* proportion of their income in tax than those on lower incomes! For instance, a single person earning £12,000 a year could be paying a slightly higher proportion of income in tax than someone *earning twice as much*

(assuming that they both had mortgages). Effectively, the structure is proportional rather than progressive over the income range containing most taxpayers.

At the bottom of the earnings scale, the structure of NIC exemptions and reduced rate brackets produce a series of little 'poverty traps' – the spikes in Figure 7a – which affect many part-time workers (largely women) – often making it not worth their while to increase hours or earnings.

A progressive structure for NICs

It would be relatively straightforward to transform employee NICs into a progressive system of taxation. The key elements would be the abolition of the Upper Earnings Limit (so that those on high earnings no longer had the top part of their earnings exempted from the charge) and the transformation of the Lower Earnings Limit into an *allowance* (or zero rate band – see Section 6) rather than an exemption. The reduced rates would be swept away in such a change, after which contributions would become simply 9% of the excess of earnings over the Lower Earnings Limit (less any of the rebates from contracting out of SERPS which would still apply up to the older upper limit; the reduction in contribution rate for certain married women could also be maintained).

Such a change by itself would not, however, be revenue neutral. In order to raise the same amount as current arrangements, the main rate would have to rise to 9.85%.[2] The distributional effects of such a combination would be that those with earnings up to about £17,000 would gain, while those above it would lose. As well as being progressive, the reform would remove the anomalies of the relationship with Income Tax.

A further reform which would improve the relationship between NICs and Income Tax (particularly within a system of independent taxation, as discussed in Section 9) would be to raise the lower limit to £50 per week to equal the single allowance for Income Tax (£2,605 a year). To achieve this within a progressive structure while raising the same total amount of revenue would require a contribution rate of 10.3%. The distributional effects of this are shown in Figure 7b. Break-even earnings would fall slightly to £16,460 (just above the current upper limit), while those on 'average' earnings of £12,700 would gain about £2 per week. Overall, 46% of all tax units would gain, while 12% would lose (the rest do not pay NICs).

The resulting combined structure of Income Tax (at current rates) and reformed NICs is shown in Figure 7c. The oddities of Figure 7a are eliminated (although the wide basic rate band still results in a flattening out of the average rate schedule; a combination of this reform of NICs and a graduated structure of Income Tax is described in Section 20). The increase in the lower limit would also have an effect on benefit entitlement (see below), which would have to be considered.

Such a structure for NICs could, of course, be used to raise more revenue than now, simply by increasing the contribution rate. For instance, raising the rate to 10.9% (on earnings above £50 per week) would result in a net increase in revenues of about £1 billion. Compared with the current system, those with earnings below about £14,900 would be gaining, but those above would now be losing.

Integration of Income Tax and NICs

The peculiarity of the structure shown in Figure 7a has led to suggestions that Income Tax and NICs should not just be aligned in the way proposed above, but actually **integrated** in some way so that there would be just one tax, rather than two. The simplest way to do this would be to abolish employee NICs altogether and increase Income Tax rates to compensate. If this was done by raising both basic and higher Income Tax rates by the same amount, they would have to increase by nearly 10 percentage points, to 34.7% and 49.7% respectively. In general, this would be progressive. Looking at income groups as a whole, as with the alignment of Income Tax and NICs shown in Figure 7b, only the richest tenth of the population would lose.

However, while the rest of the income distribution would gain *on average* (in fact, rather more than in the case shown in Figure 7b), a significant proportion of them would lose. Overall, while about half of all families would gain from integration, the number losing would be 22% – some of them from the bottom half of the income distribution.

The reason for these possibly unexpected effects lies in the differences between the *base* for Income Tax and that for NICs. NICs are only charged on earnings. Income Tax is charged on investment income and, very importantly, on pensions as well. NICs are on an *individual* basis, while Income Tax is at present calculated for many married couples on a *joint* basis (see Section 8). A wide range of deductions – mortgage interest, pension contributions and other concessions for particular activities – are allowed in calculating Income Tax, but not in calculating NICs. On the other hand, various *fringe benefits*, such as an estimate of the value of company cars, are included in the Income Tax base but are not subject to NICs, and there are special provisions in the structure of NICs relating to the self-employed, certain married women and those contracted out of SERPS which are not mirrored in Income Tax. Finally, Income Tax is calculated and runs on an *annual* basis, while NICs work on a *weekly* or *monthly* basis. As a result, someone with income in only part of the year will be able to set a whole year's Income Tax allowances against it, but the calculation of NICs will not allow for the weeks when there were no earnings.

Bringing the two taxes together therefore involves much wider distributional changes than those implied by the differences in their rate structures. It is for such reasons that the Government rejected the idea of integration in its 1986 Green Paper on *The Reform of Personal Taxation*.[3] Schemes proposed for integration have therefore usually stopped short of a full merger, but have incorpo-

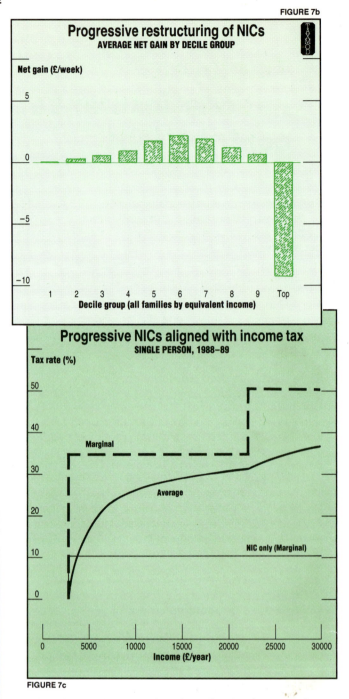

Progressive restructuring of NICs
AVERAGE NET GAIN BY DECILE GROUP

Net gain (£/week)

Decile group (all families by equivalent income)

Progressive NICs aligned with income tax
SINGLE PERSON, 1988–89

Tax rate (%)

Marginal

Average

NIC only (Marginal)

Income (£/year)

FIGURE 7c

rated devices such as a reduced rate for pensioners equivalent to the current basic rate, and so on.[4] Reform is more likely to take the form of bringing the two taxes into line in various ways – as in Figure 7c – rather than full-scale integration.

A final issue to be borne in mind is the historic role of NICs as 'insurance contributions'. This has two effects. First, NICs appear to arouse rather less antagonism than Income Tax – they are seen as going to a better cause than Income Tax because of their role in funding benefits like the basic pension. This 'public relations' advantage would be lost if the two taxes were integrated. The resulting jump in the basic rate of Income Tax might be remembered longer than the end of NICs. Second, NICs are part of the system used to determine eligibility to the 'contributory' benefits. Without a separate contribution system, this eligibility would have to depend on Income Tax records, or the contributory principle would have to be ended. This raises questions which are beyond the scope of this book, such as whether the principle is a useful part of the structure of benefits – giving some of them legitimacy and hence improving take-up – or whether it is damaging – excluding certain groups from eligibility and thus leaving them dependent on means-tested benefits.

8. Taxation of husband and wife: now and 1990

Taxing married couples raises problems which cannot be solved in a wholly satisfactory way. To understand why this is so, consider three objectives which an income tax system could meet:

■ It should be *progressive,* with people on higher incomes paying a larger proportion of their income in tax than those with lower incomes.

■ It should be *neutral towards marriage,* – that is, a couple's tax bill should not change simply because they choose to get married.

■ A married couple's tax bill should be *independent of the distribution of income between them* and should depend simply on their combined income.

It is, however, impossible to design a tax system which meets all three objectives. The first means that the proportion of a single person's income of £10,000 taken in tax should be less than the proportion taken if income was £20,000. Neutrality towards marriage would then mean that the tax taken from a couple where one earned £20,000 and the other nothing would be *higher* than that taken from a couple each earning £10,000. But this violates the third objective, as the tax bill will then depend on who received the income.

The UK system until 1990

All systems for taxing married couples therefore have to compromise on one or other of these objectives. The current UK Income Tax system is no exception; nor is the new system to be introduced in 1990 (see below). At its roots the old system is a *joint* taxation system, with the incomes of husband and wife added together for tax purposes. Notoriously, the legislation is based on the principle that, 'A woman's income chargeable to income tax shall . . . be deemed to be his [her husband's] income and not to be her income'.[1] In recognition of his presumed dependent wife, the husband receives the **Married Man's Allowance** (MMA) – more than half as large again as the personal allowance for a single person.

Originally, the system (with no wife's earnings allowance) met the objective of taxing couples equally regardless of how income was split between them. However, it meant that married women received no tax-free allowance to set against their own earnings, discouraging them from seeking work by comparison with single people. To remove this problem, the **Wife's Earned Income Allowance** was introduced and has been equal to the single personal allowance since 1942. As a result, however, a couple's tax bill *does* depend on whether the wife has earnings and hence on the distribution of income between them.

Even so, the tax on a wife's earnings can exceed that on a single person because the couple's joint income might bring them into the higher rate band. In this case they can make the **wife's earnings election,** sacrificing the advantage of the Married Man's Allowance, but with the woman's earnings taxed as if she was a single person. Whether this is worthwhile is complicated to work out, and only a minority of relatively well-off couples find it so. Note that even under this option the couple's *investment income* remains taxed jointly as part of the husband's income.

Finally, on top of a single allowance, single parents receive the **Additional Personal Allowance** (APA), set so that the total tax allowance they get equals the MMA (the APA is thus £1,490 in 1988-89).

The personal allowances received by different family types (which are what is most important in determining tax liability, given that most people are within the wide basic rate band) are therefore as follows:

Single person	£2,605 per year
Married couple where woman has no earnings	£4,095 per year
Single parent	£4,095 per year
Two-earner couple (with both MMA and wife's earned income allowance)	£6,700 per year

A couple where only the *woman* has earnings (the 'breadwinner wife') also receives total allowances of £6,700, and is more favourably treated than a couple where only the man has earnings.

The 1990 reforms

In April 1990 a new system of Income Tax for married couples will be introduced. Described as 'independent taxation', the new system will maintain the effect that an additional tax allowance will be paid to most married men simply as a result of being married.

Under the new system, spouses will be taxed separately on their incomes (from *both* earnings and investments) and each will receive a single allowance. There will also be a new **Married Couple's Allowance** (MCA), which will go to the husband (unless he does not have enough income to use it up, when it will be transferred to the wife). The level of the MCA will be set to equal the difference between what would have been the Married Man's Allowance (which will be abolished) and the single allowance. Thus, if the new system was in operation in 1988-89, the MCA would be set at £1,490 per year (the £4,095 MMA minus the £2,605 single allowance).

The first thing to note is that for the vast majority of taxpayers, the reform will make no difference to their tax bills. This is because under the new system the total allowance for couples where only the man has income will remain at £4,095 (his single allowance plus the new MCA at 1988-89 levels) and that for two-earner couples will remain at £6,700 (two single allowances plus the MCA). For most such couples, the constant allowances mean no change in their tax bills.

Nonetheless, there will be important differences:

■ Tax liability will become legally separate and the notorious deeming of her income to be his will be abolished. Married women will become entitled to more privacy in their tax affairs.

■ Both spouses will have their own basic rate band, rather than having their incomes aggregated when calculating their liability to higher rate tax. Some couples who would otherwise pay higher rate tax will no longer do so.

■ As a corollary, the higher paid two-earner couples who currently sacrifice the extra part of the married man's allowance in order to reduce their higher rate liability (see 'wife's earnings election') will not have to sacrifice the new MCA to achieve the same result.

■ The independent taxation will apply to *investment* income as well as earnings (which are effectively separately taxed already – as far as the basic rate is concerned – for most couples, thanks to the Wife's Earned Income Allowance). Women who do not have enough (or any) earnings to use up their allowance will now be able to have income like dividends from shares (but not bank or building society interest – see below) set against it. Further, some investment income now taxed at the husband's higher rate will be taxed at the wife's basic rate.

■ Two other changes will ensure that married couples will always be more favourably taxed than unmarried couples. First, the £30,000 limit on the size of mortgage eligible for tax relief has been limited to one mortgage per dwelling (for new mortgages since August 1988), rather than one per taxpayer. Before this, unmarried couples could claim relief on mortgages up to £60,000; married couples could not.

■ Secondly, an unmarried couple with two or more children can currently *both* claim the Additional Personal Allowance (both registering as 'single parents'), giving them more allowances than a married couple. This will now be ruled out.

The distributional effects of introducing this reform (if it had been implemented in 1988-89) are shown in Figure 8a. The overall cost would be just over £600 million[2] (on the assumption – disputed below – that wealthy couples do not further lower their tax by changing which of them owns their assets). More than half of this gain goes to families in the top 10% of the income distribution (indeed, £250 million would go to the top 5%). Overall, 7% of families gain and 1% lose; the vast majority is unaffected.

FIGURE 8a

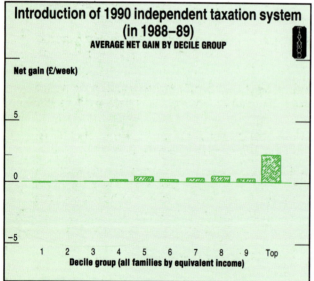

This may be a surprise to those who expected independent taxation to be progressive. It happens because two groups benefit most: couples where the wife has investment income currently taxed at the husband's higher rate (those gaining most being one-earner couples where the wife has substantial investment income); and higher paid two-earner couples who currently sacrifice the MMA and will no longer have to do so.

Although some pensioner couples with small amounts of investment income and those where the wife receives a pension as a result of her husband's contributions will gain from the change, the bulk of the gain therefore goes to those with high earnings or investment income. Furthermore, thanks to the 'composite rate' system (see Section

12), couples where the wife's only income is bank or building society interest will *not* benefit from the new allowance she receives in her own right. The losers mainly consist of the 'breadwinner wives' who were receiving 2.5 single allowances under the current system, but who will now receive only the single allowance plus MCA (they will be protected from immediate cash losses under 'transitional protection' arrangements).

Problems with the 1990 reforms

These reforms will remove much sexist legislation. Nonetheless, a special allowance (the MCA) will remain, payable almost exclusively to men simply by virtue of their being married. This tax expenditure is equivalent to a *Married Man's Benefit* of £7.16 per week (for basic rate taxpayers) or £11.46 per week (for 40% taxpayers), but worth nothing to non-taxpayers. As it is payable regardless of responsibilities (such as children or caring for elderly relatives), it is very poorly 'targeted'. There is not even an option for couples to choose to split it between them.

The new system is not designed to achieve *neutrality* in the tax treatment of marriage, but to ensure that the tax system positively favours married couples as against unmarried ones.

The transition to the new system overwhelmingly favours higher income families. Much of the gain accrues to those with substantial investment income. This contrasts with options for independent taxation which had been previously proposed under which the Married Man's Allowance would be abolished and the revenue used to increase benefits like Child Benefit.

The cost of the new system will almost certainly be greater than the £600 million mentioned above. This is because couples will, for instance, be able to transfer the ownership of shares so as to ensure that the dividends go to the spouse with an unused allowance or liable to basic rather than higher rate tax. In contrast to the independent taxation systems of other countries, the government is introducing no special anti-avoidance provisions to block this loophole. For instance, Capital Gains Tax will not be payable when assets are transferred between spouses (this also allows avoidance of large amounts of Capital Gains Tax – see Section 12).

While such transfers may mean a more equal distribution of wealth between rich men and rich women (if the former are enticed by the tax saving to give up control of the wealth), the beneficiaries from such manoeuvres will again be families with the highest incomes.

A final point to note is the interaction with a graduated rate structure of the kind described in Section 5. The cost of the 1990 reform will be limited because most taxpayers are liable only at the basic rate and because the top rate is only 40%. This limits the extent to which tax rates on husband and wife will differ. Under a graduated system the two would differ more often. More couples would gain from independent taxation and their gains would be larger. For example, introducing independent taxation of this kind into the graduated tax structure described in Figures 5b and 5c would have a net cost of £950 million, rather than £600 million.[3]

9. Taxation of husband and wife: alternatives

As explained in the previous section, the 1990 reforms will not remove some of the current problems with the taxation of husband and wife. In particular, the Married Couple's Allowance , paid primarily to married men simply because they are married, will remain an outdated anomaly. This section therefore looks at alternatives to the 1990 system, looking first at the systems in other countries.

Systems elsewhere: joint taxation

The table below summarises the systems in use in thirteen other OECD countries. Five of the countries use **joint** taxation systems. Under such systems, married couples are taxed as a single unit, with their incomes added together and the same tax charged regardless of which spouse received it. Two of these, France and West Germany, use a 'split' or 'quotient' system (see box), while in the others, the **tax schedule** (structure of allowances and rate bands) for married couples differs – with wider rate bands, for instance – from that applying to single people.

One problem with joint taxation systems is that they are cumbersome to administer, as the tax on one spouse depends on the income of the other. A second is that they generally involve a disincentive for the second spouse – in practical terms, usually the wife – to take paid work. This was a major problem with the Government's original proposals for introducing a system of **transferable allowances** (see box).

The problem is that the couple effectively receives all its tax allowances against the income of the *first* spouse. When the second spouse has income, all of this will be taxed, with no tax-free slice. Tax starts at once, which is why this problem is known as the **'threshold' effect.** As a result, married women deciding whether to take paid employment will face more tax than a single person in the same position. This may have important effects: research on the labour supply effects of taxation suggests that this decision is the most sensitive to taxation.[1]

'Split' or 'quotient' systems of joint taxation

An example of these is the French system.[2] There the incomes of the whole family are added together and then the total is split into a number of *parts* reflecting family size – two for a married couple plus a half for each child (except for the third child who counts as a whole part). Thus a married couple with three children and an income of F300,000 would have their income split into three parts of F100,000. Each of these would be taxed at the same rate as a single person with an income of F100,000.

This kind of system is very generous towards married couples, particularly those with several children. One result is that the French income tax system cannot raise very much revenue without imposing very high tax rates on single people. This may explain why France puts so much reliance on its extensive system of individually based social security contributions (see Section 4). A second result is that the rich benefit more in respect of their children than the poor.

Transferable allowances

Before the Government announced its actual plans for 1990, it published two 'Green Papers' on possible reforms for family taxation.[3] The second of these focused on the idea of **transferable allowances.**

Under these, all married couples where both spouses had income would receive the equivalent of two single allowances (not 2.5 as now and in 1990). Spouses without income to use their own allowance would transfer all of it (under 'fully transferable allowances') or part of it (under 'partially transferable allowances') to their partners.

These would have had several disadvantages, which the actual 1990 reform has avoided:

■ They would have been administratively complicated, particularly where one spouse stopped or started earning during the year.

■ The system would *not* have been independent – the tax on one spouse would depend on the income of the other.

■ They would have involved a threshold effect (especially with fully transferable allowances).

■ *Either* there would have been large losses for two-earner couples (with their allowances cut) *or* the reform would have been very expensive (with all allowances increased to protect the two-earner couples).

Family taxation systems in thirteen countries

Fully independent taxation (with concessions for one-earner couples)
Australia
Canada
Italy
New Zealand

Independent taxation of earnings; joint taxation of investment income
Denmark
Japan (small amounts of investment income taxed separately; concession for one-earner couples)
Netherlands (with concession for one-earner couples)
Sweden

Joint taxation – 'Split' or 'Quotient' System
France
West Germany

Joint taxation – Special rate schedules for married couples
Ireland (joint taxation as option)
USA (different rate schedules for married couples filing together or filing separately)

Joint taxation – Same rate schedule for single and married
Belgium (Splitting system for those with incomes below limit)

SOURCES: *The Reform of Personal Taxation*, Cmnd 9756, HMSO, London, 1986; National sources.

Systems elsewhere: independent taxation

Eight of the countries use some form of **independent** taxation (of which the 1990 British system will be a variant) under which married people are taxed separately, as if both were single. However, four of these have independent taxation of earnings, but joint taxation of investment income (which avoids the tax avoidance possibilities from married couples rearranging assets between themselves which result from fully independent taxation). Six of the countries give special concessions to one-earner couples. None of them gives a concession to *all* married couples in the way that the current and 1990 British systems do.

Should there be concessions for one-earner couples?

As joint taxation systems involve both administrative complication and 'threshold' effects, there are good reasons for what appears to be an international move away from joint taxation and towards independent taxation. This raises its own problems, in particular whether any special provision should be made for one-earner couples, in order to tax them less than a single person with the same amount of income. There are two reasons why one might want to do this. The first is the principle that a couple is not as well off as a single person with the same income and so should be taxed less. The second is pragmatic: they receive a concession now and should not suffer losses from its removal.

The principle of favouring one-earner couples *per se* amounts to saying – in the majority of cases – that the husband should be given favourable tax treatment in recognition of a dependent wife. One then has to ask *why* she is dependent on him. The strength of the argument may be very different depending on whether there are, for instance, children being cared for. But in this case it is the children that create the case for favourable treatment, not the fact that only one member of the couple is earning.

If there is special treatment of *one*-earner couples, a dilemma arises. If an *equivalent* concession is not given to two-earner couples, a threshold effect is created. On the other hand, if two-earner couples are also favoured, the cost to the Government is increased and a benefit is passed to those who do not need it (as with the Married Man's Allowance, or the new Married Couple's Allowance).

The conclusion drawn by the great majority of those who responded to the Government's Green Papers[4] was that the balance of the arguments favours fully independent taxation with no special allowances for married couples. Instead, the Married Man's Allowance (or Married Couple's Allowance from 1990) should be abolished (or phased out), with the revenue used to increase benefits like Child Benefit and allowances paid to those caring for the elderly or disabled people. Instead of the indiscriminate 'Married Man's Benefit' introduced by the 1990 reforms, the concessions should be concentrated on those with a clear need for them.

The effect of abolishing the Married Man's Allowance

The simplest proposal is that the Married Man's Allowance (MMA) (or Married Couple's Allowance (MCA) after 1990) should be abolished for non-pensioners (pensioners are considered separately – see box on facing page), with the revenue spent on doubling Child Benefit from its present £7.25 to £14.50 per week. This would mean that no couple with children and paying tax at the basic rate would lose (as the £1,490 additional part of the MMA is worth £7.16 per week, and the extra Child Benefit for just one child would compensate).

If this was done within the current tax system, the net cost would be about £340 million (abolishing the MMA does not quite pay for doubling Child Benefit).[5] If it was done at the same time as introducing independent taxation of all income (that is, the 1990 system without the MCA), the net effect would be a revenue cost of £800 million (just £200 million more than the introduction of the 1990 reform by itself).

It would, overall, be progressive, with (starting from the current tax treatment of husband and wife) the bottom 60% of families gaining on average and the top 20% losing (the rest roughly breaking even). The gains right at the bottom would, however, be limited by the way in which means-tested benefits work (see Section 10). By itself, a rise in Child Benefit is of no value to most of those on Income Support – it would be offset by an equivalent cut in benefit. Similarly, some others would lose up to 85% of the net gain from increased Child Benefit in reduced Housing Benefit. Family Credit is rather different – left to itself, payments would *rise* as a result of the abolition of the MMA (and hence lower net income after allowing for tax), but it would not be affected directly by the change in Child Benefit (although there could be indirect effects through the formula that the Government uses to set Family Credit rates).

Married man's allowance abolished for non-pensioners, child benefit doubled
AVERAGE NET GAIN BY DECILE GROUP

Net gain (£/week)

Decile group (all families by equivalent income)

This presents a dilemma. There are good arguments for using universal benefits like Child Benefit to 'float' families off means-tested benefits. However, making no equivalent change to, say, Income Support rates would mean that some of the poorest families who have lost out most in recent years would gain nothing. The package examined in Figure 9a therefore involves a compromise under which (within the current system for taxing husband and wife) the MMA is abolished for non-pensioners and Income Support, Family Credit and Housing Benefit rates are adjusted so that roughly *half* the increase in Child Benefit accrues to non-taxpaying benefit recipients (a gain of £3.75 per child under 10 on IS, for instance), while the other half has the 'floating-off' effect (with 13% fewer Family Credit claimants after the reform, for instance). A side effect of this reform is that the Income Support rate for children under 10 would become £14.50, equal to Child Benefit, so that support for these children would be equalised for people on and off IS (and could then be taken out of the IS calculation altogether, except where there were special needs to consider).

The benefit adjustment increases the net cost of the

reform to £635 million (starting from the current treatment of husband and wife). As the figure shows, the gains are now evenly spread through the bottom 60% of the income distribution. Overall, 23% of families gain, with 15% losing (the other 'families' are single people or pensioners).

Independent taxation without a Married Couple's Allowance

Figure 9b shows the effects of the combination of introducing fully independent taxation as proposed for 1990, but without an MCA for either pensioners or non-pensioners, while doubling Child Benefit, increasing the married pension by £11.90 and adjusting Income Support, Housing Benefit and Family Credit in the ways described above and in the box on the treatment of pensioners.

The net cost of the reform would be £2,150 million, that is, £1,550 million more than that of introducing the 1990 system by itself (with pensioners as a group being the main net beneficiaries, for the reasons explained in the box). The benefits of this additional spending are distributed very progressively (as can be seen by comparing Figures 8a and 9b). 34% of families would gain while 15% would lose (again, the other 'families' include single people).

FIGURE 9b

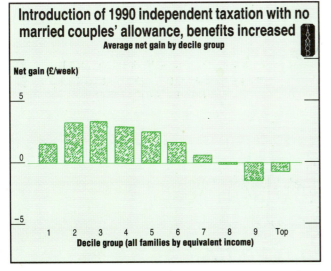

Although progressive overall, some of the losers are not on high incomes: 5% of the bottom 60% lose (although 40% of them gain). These losers are non-pensioner childless taxpaying couples, losing £7.16 per week from the abolition of the MMA. There are three approaches which could be taken which would ameliorate such losses:

■ The reform could be combined with a progressive restructuring of Income Tax rates and NICs (see Sections 5 and 7), which would give offsetting gains to many, especially those with below average earnings.

■ Certain married couples – say, those where the wife is aged over 50 at the time of the change – could retain the right to the MMA to protect them from unforeseen losses (the rationale being that the expectations of such couples are less likely to include the wife's participation in the labour market). On retirement, they would be switched to the pensioner system (see box) and the concession would eventually die out (a process known in the USA as 'grandfathering' or as 'red-circling' in union circles).

■ The reform could be *phased in*. For instance, the *cash* value of the MMA (or the total of single allowance and MCA in the 1990 system) could be frozen until the single allowance caught up with it (or the MCA disappeared). For instance, if the MMA had been frozen at its 1982-83 level

of £2445, it would have disappeared by 1987-88. This would, of course, delay the revenues to finance an increase in benefits; but it would prevent any sudden cash increases in tax bills.

The effects of some of these concessions, and of the complex interactions between abolishing the MMA or MCA and reforms suggested in other sections are included in the reform proposal discussed in Section 20.

Independent taxation, pensioners and the age allowance

Pensioners receive special treatment in the Income Tax system. Instead of the £2,605 single allowance, single people aged between 65 and 79 are entitled to an **age allowance** of £3,180 (those aged 80 or over have an allowance of £3,310). Where one member of a couple is aged 65 or more, the man's allowance is £5,035 (or £5,205 if one is 80 or over). These allowances are gradually reduced to the level of the ordinary allowances for those whose income exceeds £10,600. Under the 1990 reforms, the essence of this structure will be maintained, with, for instance, a Married Couple's Allowance of £1,855 (rather than the normal £1,490) where the older spouse is aged between 65 and 79. Married women aged over 65 will receive the age allowance in their own right and will be taxed separately.[6]

This system is rather strange.[7] The additional allowance is worth nothing to the many pensioners who do not pay tax. To taxpayers (below the income limit), the addition is worth up to £2.76 per week (single) or £4.52 per week (married man). Its main rationale seems to be the administrative advantage of keeping pensioners with little income beside the state pension out of the tax net. As a way of helping pensioners, it would be more progressive to spend the resources foregone by the concession (£450 million in 1987-88)[8] on increasing the basic pension. If carried out at zero net cost, this would, however, mean losses for taxpaying pensioners (as *all* pensioners would gain from the pension increase, but only *some* receive the age allowance now). To protect taxpaying single pensioners from a loss resulting from the abolition of age allowance would, for instance, require a £3.68 increase in the single pension (worth £2.76 after tax). This would significantly increase the net cost of the change.

Abolition of the age allowance altogether is considered further in Section 20. As far as this section is concerned, the analogy with abolishing the non-pensioner Married Man's Allowance and increasing Child Benefit would be to reduce the married age allowance to the single age allowance while increasing the married pension. For those aged between 65 and 79, the drop in allowance from £5,035 to £3,180 would require an increase of £11.90 per week in the married pension to prevent losses for taxpayers.

The increase in the pension would, of course, benefit non-taxpayers but would also alter their entitlements to means-tested benefits. Again, it might be thought appropriate for *half* of the increase in pension to be reflected in Income Support rates (for instance through a £5.95 increase in the Income Support premium for pensioner couples).

The cost of this reform would depend on the starting system of taxation. Within the current system for taxing husband and wife, the cost would be about £450 million.[9] However, if the starting point was the 1990 system of independent taxation, it would be twice as expensive (a net cost of £900 million for pensioners as a whole). This is because the wife's part of the married pension would then be taxed as her income, which in many cases would be below the single age allowance.

10. Tax and social security

The tax and social security systems have grown up independently, producing unplanned interactions of which the 'poverty trap' is the best known. Social security is divided into two not very well co-ordinated parts. The first is the **national insurance** system, generally credited to the 1942 Beveridge Report. National insurance benefits – the state retirement pension, Unemployment Benefit and Invalidity Benefit – are paid regardless of income to people in particular *categories* – being retired, unemployed or sick. They depend on whether someone has paid[1] National Insurance Contributions (NICs). Those who do not have a 'full contribution record' do not receive full benefit – indeed, they may not be entitled at all.

The social security budget

The table shows planned spending on benefits in 1988-89 and in 1978-79 (at 1988-89 prices and adjusted onto a consistent basis). The most important shift revealed is the much faster growth in the means-tested benefits than the others, rising from 15% of benefit expenditure in 1978-79 to 28% a decade later. This has not occurred because means-tested benefits have become more generous in relation to overall living standards: with the exception of Family Credit, benefits have become relatively less generous. Rather, the growth of unemployment and in the size of the retired population have put more families in the income ranges where they are eligible for means-tested help; benefits like the retirement pension or Unemployment Benefit have not been generous enough by themselves to keep recipients above the minimum income guaranteed by Income Support.

Social security spending 1978-79 and 1988-89[2]
(£ million at 1988-89 prices)

	1978-79	1988-89	Growth 78/9 to 88/9 (%)
Non-means tested			
Pensions	18,630	21,410	15
Child Benefit[1]	5,300	4,700	−11
Injury, sickness, disability[2]	4,570	6,950	52
Unemployment Benefit	1,380	1,530	11
Other family	320	230	−29
Total	30,200	34,820	15
Means-tested benefits			
Income Support[3]	3,500	9,080	159
Housing Benefit[4]	1,950	4,190	115
Family Credit[5]	50	460	794
Total	5,500	13,730	149
Administration	1,600	2,240	40
Total	37,300	50,790	36

1. Includes equivalent of Child Tax Allowances in 1978-79.
2. Includes estimated cost of Statutory Sick Pay in 1988-89.
3. Supplementary Benefit excluding rent of recipients in 1978-79.
4. Includes rent of SB recipients in 1978-79.
5. Family Income Supplement in 1978-79.

Child Benefit has some similarities with national insurance benefits in that its payment depends only on having a child and not on income, but it is truly **universal,** not depending on contributions, as is One Parent Benefit, paid to single parents. Mobility Allowance and Attendance Allowance are also non-contributory and non-means-tested, depending only on circumstances.

The second part of social security consists of the **means-tested benefits** such as Income Support, Family Credit and Housing Benefit. These were reformed in April 1988 following the Fowler reviews of social security, but share many characteristics with their predecessors (Supplementary Benefit, Family Income Supplement and the old system of Housing Benefit). Entitlement depends crucially on income level: as it rises, benefit falls. It also depends on family composition, and other factors such as housing costs or age, but *not* on contributions.

The problem of take-up

A key difference between means-tested and other benefits is in the proportions of those entitled to them who actually claim them. The Government says that take-up for the contributory benefits, like the retirement pension, widow's benefits and Unemployment Benefit is 'close to 100%'; for Child Benefit it is 'virtually 100%'; and for the non-means-tested One Parent Benefit take-up was 93% in 1984.[3]

For the means-tested benefits, take-up is much lower. Measured by the numbers of those entitled who claim, 'case-load take-up' was 76% for Supplementary Benefit (1983), 77% for Housing Benefit (1984) and for Family Income Supplement it was only 54% (1983 and 1984). Measured by the amount of cash available which was claimed ('expenditure take-up'), the respective figures were 89%, 88% and 65% (those entitled to larger amounts of benefit are more likely to claim).

The structure of means-tested benefits

The oldest of these is *Income Support* (IS), descended from Supplementary Benefit and National Assistance. It is also the simplest in basic principle: it is intended to ensure that families not in full-time work do not fall below a certain level of income – the 'personal allowance' reflecting family composition, plus any 'premium' (such as for being a pensioner) and any other addition they might be entitled to. Income Support thus makes up the difference between income from other sources and this level.[4] If pre-benefit income is £1 higher, Income Support is £1 lower. It therefore embodies a 100% **taper** or 'effective marginal tax rate' on additional income.

Income Support is not payable to those who are in paid work for 24 hours or more per week. They may be entitled to Family Credit if they have children and a low income. An amount depending on family size is payable as Family Credit if net income (after allowing for income tax and NICs, etc.) is below a certain 'applicable amount'. Above it, Family Credit is cut by 70 pence for every extra £1 of net income.

Housing Benefit has a similar structure. If net income (allowing for income tax, NICs, Child Benefit *and* Family Credit) is at or below the family's Income Support rate, benefit equals 100% of rent plus 80% of rates. For every £1 by which net income rises above this, benefit is reduced by 65 pence for rent and 20 pence for rates.

Figure 10a shows a simplified version of how entitlement varies with earnings for a couple with 2 children (both aged 11-15), rent of £20 per week and rates of £8 per week (assuming only the man has earnings).[5] Changing any of these assumptions would affect the detailed picture, but the overall shape would be the same.

Tax cuts and benefits

A side effect of the April 1988 reforms was that Housing Benefit and Family Credit became based on *net* income after allowing for Income Tax and NICs. This means that if tax is reduced, the net income taken into account for this calculation rises and benefits will be reduced. For someone receiving both Family Credit and Housing Benefit, only 4.5 pence in every £1 of a tax cut would actually benefit them financially; for someone on Family Credit alone, only 30 pence out of every £1 (although this adjustment may not happen immediately.)

The poverty trap

In the example in Figure 10a, if gross weekly earnings rise from £30.40 (when Housing Benefit starts to fall) to £165.90 (when Family Credit runs out), net income only rises from £126.20 to £143.70. An earnings rise of £135.50 increases net income by only £17.50 – equivalent to facing a marginal tax rate of 87% over the whole income range. This constitutes what has become known as the **poverty trap** – the position in which it is very hard to make any difference to one's standard of living by earning more (although it should be remembered that in the *short term* benefits may not change immediately even if earnings do).

Much concern with the poverty trap has focused on *incentives* – why should people work harder or seek promotion if they would gain hardly any net income? Such effects may be hard to find at the tax rates paid by the majority of the population, but marginal rates approaching 100% may be more of a problem. There are two other reasons for concern. The first is *equity*. Is it *fair* that someone who earns £150 per week should be hardly any better off than someone earning £50 per week? Indeed, over some income ranges in the past (and, in certain circumstances, even now) those with higher earnings could be worse off than those with lower. The second is the problem of *cheating*. The gain from hiding income is much higher for those in the poverty trap than for those only facing Income Tax and NICs.

Exactly how the poverty trap affects those on low earnings depends on where they start from and on the increase in earnings being considered. Figure 10b shows the marginal tax rates for small earnings increases for the same example. The spikes in the diagram mark the points at which the jumps in NIC liabilities occur (see Section 7) and at which Family Credit and the rent and rates components of Housing Benefit fall below the 50 pence per week minimum payments (at which point entitlement disappears altogether). Otherwise, the highest marginal rate is for someone on Family Credit and Housing Benefit, paying NICs at 7% and Income Tax at 25%; here the marginal tax rate adds up to nearly 97% – 97 pence out of every extra £1 of earnings is lost!

These marginal rates on *low* earners exceeding 80% compare with those shown in Figure 7c for those with higher incomes, with a maximum marginal rate of 40%. While the 1988 Budget abolished the top marginal rate of income tax of 60% (which would have affected 180,000 families in 1988-89),[6] the April 1988 benefit reforms increased to 545,000 the number of low income families facing marginal tax rates of *70% or more,* 255,000 more than in November 1985.[7]

This is one of the great problems of means-tested benefits. The April 1988 reforms were partly designed to remove effective marginal tax rates *above* 100%, and

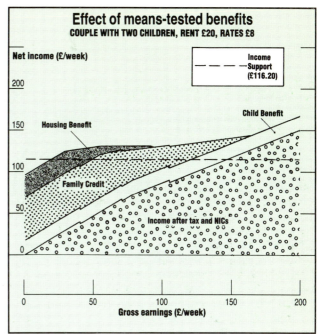

FIGURE 10a

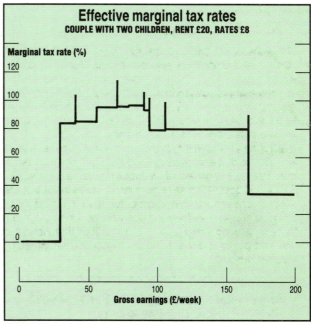

FIGURE 10b

were largely successful in doing so. The cost was, however, to widen the income range over which rates *near to* 100% apply, bringing more families into the poverty trap.

As can be seen by looking back at Figure 2c, the earnings distribution becomes much denser above £120 per week. If one looks at the distribution for men working full-time only (which may be most relevant for families in the poverty trap), while only 12% had weekly earnings below £120 in April 1987, a further 30% had earnings between £120 and £180. Historically the poverty trap has been an acute problem facing few families; it has now become a slightly less acute problem facing many more. Further, if for instance, it was decided to make the Family Credit system more generous as a cheap alternative to Child Benefit, the poverty trap would quickly extend to ranges where there are many more earners. This appears to be the course upon which the Government is set, following the freezing of Child Benefit for a second year, announced in October 1988.

11. Tax and social security: reforms

This book is not primarily about benefits; see 'Where to find out more' for CPAG publications and others which describe their operation and failings in much greater detail than would be possible here. However, the interaction between tax and benefit systems has to be addressed.

A first question is why there should be any interaction between the two systems at all. Surely people should either receive benefits *or* pay tax, with no overlap between the two? However, only charging tax on incomes above possible benefit levels for those with the greatest needs would be very expensive (or need much higher tax rates). A family with four children paying average housing costs could be entitled to Income Support and Housing Benefit of more than £7,000 per year. Raising all tax allowances to this level would be prohibitively expensive, but an overlap would remain for those with even greater needs.

The cost could be cut if tax allowances depended on individual circumstances. But this would greatly increase the information needed to calculate tax: in order to set the right allowances, employers would have to collect – and someone would have to check – new information about *everyone's* family size, housing costs and other special needs.

An overlap between taxes and benefits is, in fact, perfectly sensible. Child Benefit is currently paid through a system where no information is needed about income, while tax is paid via PAYE where no information is needed about children. This may mean that the State is 'taking with one hand while giving with the other' – or **churning,** as it has been called – but it is in many ways simpler to operate than the old system of Family Allowances and Child Tax Allowances. Under that, Income Tax depended on the number of children people had, as well as on income.

Taxing benefits

Another aspect of the overlap between taxes and benefits is the tax treatment of benefits. In some cases, there are good arguments for taxing benefits. 'Income replacement' benefits like Unemployment Benefit serve the purpose of maintaining income while it is interrupted. It is fair for these to be taxed in the same way as other income so as to avoid inequity between those receiving them for part of the year and those with only income from work.[1] Equally, means-tested benefits like Housing Benefit should not be taxed. As they now depend on income *after* tax – the system would go into perpetual motion if the tax also depended on the benefits!

In between, there are benefits which are designed to help people with extra *costs* resulting from their circumstances. Here the situation is less clear. For instance, it has been argued that Child Benefit should be increased, but made taxable (it is non-taxable now). Within the current Income Tax system this would be fairly pointless. As the overwhelming majority pays at the same basic rate, an increase of, say, a third in Child Benefit followed by making it taxable (at 25%) would leave them all in the same position. Non-taxpayers would gain, and those on higher

rates would lose a little, but the administrative cost would be too high to make it worthwhile. The situation would be rather different if there was a graduated tax structure of the kind described in Section 5.[2]

Fundamental reforms

While there is almost general agreement that there has to be some overlap, there is much less agreement about what form it should take. One proposal is that the tax and benefit systems should be **integrated,** with a single calculation made as to whether someone should receive a net benefit or pay net tax. Under one alternative – a **social dividend** or **basic income** – everyone (in the 'pure' version of the scheme) would receive a certain amount of income from the State, financed through taxation of all income with no allowances. These proposals are discussed in the boxes.

Means-testing versus universalism

Part of the argument about the relationship between taxes and benefits is about administration. There is also a more fundamental issue about the extent to which benefits should be means-tested or whether they should go to all regardless of income. Some proposals for integration of tax and benefit administration also suggest that currently universal payments like Child Benefit and the state pension should only be paid to those with relatively low incomes. Social dividend proposals by contrast suggest that all payments should be universal, with no means-testing at all.[3]

The key argument *in favour* of more means-testing is exemplified by Figure 11a, showing the effect of cutting Child Benefit by £2 per week and using the savings (£1.1 billion) to increase Income Support and Family Credit (adding £7.70 to the child additions for each after adjusting the latter for the loss of Child Benefit). The figure allows for incomplete take-up of the means-tested benefits. A similar picture would be given by a switch from other universal benefits to means-tested ones.

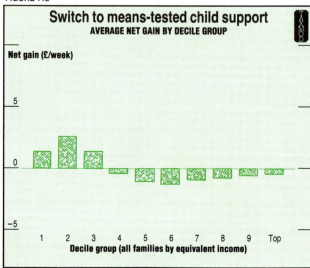

FIGURE 11a

Switch to means-tested child support
AVERAGE NET GAIN BY DECILE GROUP

Net gain (£/week)

Decile group (all families by equivalent income)

In these *overall* terms, the change is clearly progressive. The bottom 30% of the population gains at the expense of the top 70% and the gains right at the bottom are significant (after allowing for the fact that three quarters of families do not have children and are unaffected). **Targeting** through means-testing means that less is given to the 'non-poor', perhaps enabling more to be given to the poor. Universal benefits like Child Benefit are said to be 'inefficient' in that, if the aim is taken solely as poverty relief, part of spending misses its target.[4] In the case of Child Benefit the Government has calculated that almost half the amount spent goes to those with above average incomes (*after* allowing for family composition). This has been used to justify the recent Child Benefit freeze and increased emphasis on Family Credit.[5]

If this was all there was to it, greater 'targeting' would clearly be the way to go, but there are fundamental and practical objections:

■ The argument assumes that the amount available for benefits depends on a fixed amount of tax revenue. However, removing benefits from those on higher incomes reduces their net incomes as much as greater taxation: the level of taxation which is politically acceptable will be less. The idea that the whole amount 'saved' by cutting Child Benefit would be liberated for the poor is a mirage: in the long run taxes would probably end up lower as well.

■ The shape of the tax and benefit system depends on the political interplay of different interest groups. Where spending is *only* directed at the poor, the political lobby in its defence is weak. In recent years services at least partly benefiting 'the middle classes' have been much less severely cut than those where their famous 'sharp elbows' were not available in defence.[6] Under the reform in Figure 11a, 81% of families with children would lose and only 19% gain; the interests of poor families would be isolated.

■ 'Vertical' redistribution is not the only aim of benefits. One way to ensure that those with children pay less tax than those without is to give allowances like the old Child Tax Allowances. The same result is given by applying the same tax schedule to everyone, but paying Child Benefit as well. Cutting back universal payments means that this 'horizontal' redistribution is lost.

■ Another wider aim is the principle of 'social solidarity' underlying continental social insurance (and Beveridge's ideas that 'men should stand together with their fellows').[7] In our lives, we all pass through troughs of relatively low income and peaks of relative prosperity; the welfare state is intended to help us all at the points in our lives when we need it.

■ As the box about integration suggests, benefits also affect distribution *within* the family. Where, for instance, a man does not share his income equally, his wife and children may be much worse off than total family income would suggest.

■ Means-tested benefits are fundamentally *inefficient* in carrying out their objectives because *take-up* is below 100% (see Section 10). The effect of 'targeting' is that some of the 'targets' are missed altogether. In the example in Figure 11a, *a third of families in the bottom three decile groups lose because they would not receive the increased means-tested benefits to which they would be entitled* (in all, 62% of families with children in the bottom half of the distribution would lose).

■ Means-tested benefits cost more than universal benefits to administer. Administering retirement pensions cost 1.4% of the benefit expenditure in 1985-86 compared with 11.3% for Supplementary Benefit.

■ The withdrawal of benefit as incomes rise is equivalent to a tax on additional income, in its extreme form causing the poverty trap. Further means-testing would exacerbate this. For instance, the change in Figure 11a would nearly double the number of families receiving Family Credit with its 70% withdrawal rate, and the numbers facing total marginal tax rates above 70% would rise by a half. A lower

Integration of taxes and benefits

Someone with 2 children earning £85 per week could be paying NICs and Income Tax while claiming Family Credit and Housing Benefit (see Figure 10a). Their employer would first calculate tax on the basis of earnings. The DSS would then calculate Family Credit and the council Housing Benefit, both on the basis of wageslips. Three separate calculations would be carried out to arrive at the family's net income.

It has been argued that this is obviously absurd and it would be much better for there to be one integrated calculation with a single net payment made – an addition to wages if benefit exceeds tax, or a deduction if tax is larger. Not only could this save administration, but the system could also be designed to avoid the worst of the poverty trap. In one model, benefits would be replaced by a **negative income tax** with a similar calculation made for everyone, but those below the tax threshold would *receive* a payment rather than making one.

On a closer examination the case for integration is not so strong. First, the number of people affected by the worst of the overlap is small. Only about 200,000 people used to receive FIS. Although more will be entitled to Family Credit, the number of recipients – the Government's initial estimate was 470,000 for 1988-89[8] – will remain very small compared with 20 million taxpayers. The majority of those receiving Housing Benefit are pensioners and the unemployed, not those with earnings. To redesign the PAYE system so that employers collected information on *everyone's* family size and housing costs would result in much more unnecessary effort than the current duplication of effort in income assessment.[9]

A second problem was highlighted by the reforms which introduced Family Credit. Originally the Government suggested that it should be integrated with PAYE and that payment should be made 'through the wage packet', thus saving the DSS – and claimants – the effort of a second income assessment. There was a successful campaign against this on the grounds that it would mean a shift from payments which had been made to the main carer (usually women) under FIS to ones which would go to the main earner (usually men) through the wage packet. It was feared that this would leave women in families where income was not equally shared worse off.

Thirdly, tax and benefit assessments do different jobs. Income Tax is assessed on an *annual* basis – this is fair, in that it avoids the extra burden which a progressive rate structure would impose on those whose incomes fluctuate during the year. By contrast, the need for benefits has to be assessed over a short period, say a week. If someone loses their job, it is not acceptable to tell them that when they go back to work their net tax payment will be lower – they need the cash *now*. But by definition, a benefit paid through the wage packet could not reach them. More generally, an integrated tax and benefit system would have difficulty coping with those moving in and out of employment during the year.

These objections relate to integrating the current tax and means-tested benefit systems. The balance of administrative advantage would look rather different if, as has also been suggested,[10] Child Benefit was replaced with a souped-up version of Family Credit which extended further up the earnings distribution; the case for integrated administration is stronger if more taxpayers are means-tested. The arguments for – and against – this kind of move are discussed in the main text.

Social dividends or basic incomes

The principle of a social dividend or basic income is simple. As explained in Section 6, for basic rate taxpayers the effect of taxing income in excess of an allowance is the same as charging tax on all income and then deducting a fixed amount, a 'tax credit'. Meanwhile, non-taxpayers are paid benefits like Income Support, which are cut back as income rises. Why not consolidate these two systems into one in which a single payment is made to all, financed by taxing *all* income, with no allowances? This system would have no poverty trap and would do away with the complications of income tax allowances and means-testing. All income could be taxed at a single rate at source.

A first problem is that current tax allowances are not large enough to give a reasonable social dividend. The £4,095 Married Man's Allowance is equivalent to a credit of less than £20 per week compared with an Income Support rate for a couple with no children of £51.45 per week plus housing costs. In order to pay a social dividend at a rate anywhere approaching Income Support levels, marginal tax rates would have to be far higher than those currently facing most people. The exact level depends on what income would be taxable; one estimate gives a range of 68% to 86%.[11] Taxpayers would, of course, gain from the social dividend offsetting this higher tax, but such high marginal rates affecting everyone raise serious incentive and evasion problems.

Faced with this difficulty, two modifications of the pure proposal have been suggested. One is for a 'modified' social dividend, with a payment close to the tax credit equivalent of existing tax allowances paid to everyone, and an additional payment made to those on low incomes. This would have a very similar effect to some of the proposals which have been made for integrating tax and benefits. A second would be to introduce a 'partial basic income', again replacing the existing tax allowances with their cash equivalent, but retaining National Insurance benefits as a first stage towards a non means-tested social dividend, but paid rather less indiscriminately than in the pure scheme. This has quite a lot in common with proposals for more reliance on 'contingent' benefits discussed in the text.

withdrawal rate could reduce the worst of the poverty trap – but only by extending it to more people.

Fundamentally, if the combined tax and benefit system *increases* the incomes of the poor and *reduces* those of the rich, there has to be slower growth of net than of gross incomes somewhere in between. The 'poverty trap' is simply the result of cramming all of this into one income range. A social dividend spreads them out evenly over the whole range.

What matters is not just the range of marginal tax rates but also the numbers affected. A key objection to more means-testing is that it would extend something close to the poverty trap to many more. The key objection to a social dividend is that it would mean high marginal tax rates for everyone. The poverty trap has evolved as a way of keeping down the marginal tax rates of most earners at the expense of very high marginal tax rates on a relatively small number.

In trying to escape this dilemma, there is another kind of information which can help. People in certain circumstances – the unemployed, sick, disabled, or retired – are more 'at risk' of having low incomes than others. The national insurance system pays benefits to those groups for precisely that reason. Similarly, One Parent Benefit and Child Benefit go to those whose needs are relatively greater. The use of such **contingent** benefits is a way of avoiding the expense of a full social dividend while minimising marginal tax rates.

Contingent benefits are not without economic effect either. Pensions alter the economic effects of retirement and of saving for retirement. Unemployment Benefit (and Income Support) reduce the gain from taking a job and have been accused of causing an 'unemployment trap', under which people may be better off out of work than in work (although research suggests that this is very uncommon).[12] In the USA, it has been suggested that 'Aid to Families with Dependent Children', which in many States is only paid to single parents, has led to family break-up.

There has been much research on both sides of the Atlantic into these 'side-effects of the welfare state', but without reaching conclusions which would shake an agnostic view. As A.B. Atkinson concluded a comprehensive review of this evidence: 'The great volume of empirical research in this field in the past decade has not led to robust and widely accepted answers to the basic question as to how income support affects economic behaviour'.[13]

A messy conclusion

This section does not provide a neat solution to the relationship between tax and benefits. Integration does not offer a magic solution to the poverty trap. More means-testing does not guarantee more resources for the poor. A universal social dividend would mean generally very high marginal tax rates. Getting rid of means-tested benefits altogether would mean losses for those on the lowest incomes unless contingent benefits had been built up to a high enough level to replace them. While that process was going on, some of those on the lowest incomes would gain nothing.

It does, however, suggest the direction in which improvements to benefits could be made. In the package of reforms described in Section 20, the emphasis is on improving the retirement pension, Child Benefit, One Parent Benefit and Unemployment Benefit by rather greater amounts than means-tested Income Support. This enables the number of people dependent on the means-tested benefit to be reduced – 'floated off' – through the faster increase in other benefits. At the same time, some of the recent changes to means-tested benefits – like the 80% maximum to rate rebates or the severity of the Housing Benefit 'tapers' – have hit those on low incomes so badly that they cannot be ignored, even though removing them extends the reach of means-testing somewhat.

12. How investment income and capital gains are taxed now

Investment income is much more unequally distributed than earned income. While the top 1% of all families received 6.4% of all income before tax in 1984-85, they received more than 12% of all investment income.[1] Looking more narrowly at those families actually paying tax, the top 5% received 16% of earned income assessed for tax in 1984-85, but 36% of investment income, including 45% of rents received and no less than 52% of UK dividends.[2] The abolition of the Investment Income Surcharge in 1980, and the benefits which will come from separate taxation of investment income in 1990 give major gains to people at the top of the income distribution. Conversely, heavier taxation of investment income would be a progressive way of financing redistribution towards the bottom half of the population. Achieving this would not, however, be straightforward.

A first problem is indicated by the following. At the end of 1984 the total value of personal wealth (the 'net worth of the personal sector') came to £1,046 billion (including the value of rights to occupational pensions, consumer durables, etc).[3] The total amount of 'investment income' assessed for tax by the Inland Revenue in 1984-85 was only £9.6 billion; with a further £3.2 billion of capital gains (assessed by October 1986), this gives a combined return of *just over 1%* on total personal wealth.[4] Given that investors could have expected a return of 10% in nominal terms (and perhaps 4% in real terms, after allowing for anticipated inflation – see box below), it is evident that most of the 'return' to wealth (that is, the flow of benefits from its ownership) does not come in the forms which are taxed as 'investment income'. Part of the reason why it does not lies in the way in which the returns on different kinds of investment are taxed.

The current treatment of investment income[5]

The key features of the tax treatment of the income and other benefits from wealth are summarised in the para-

---

Inflation and investment income

Inflation makes the measurement of investment income more difficult than it would be if there were stable prices. If prices did not change, an interest rate of 5% would mean that someone investing £100 today in a building society account could spend £5 in a year's time and still have the same level of spending power saved in the account. If prices rose by 5%, however, all £105 – the original £100 plus £5 interest – would have to be kept in the account in order for its **real** purchasing power to be left unchanged – the **real return** would actually be zero. In this situation a **nominal** interest rate of just over 10% would be needed to give a real return of 5%.

Some forms of investment – notably those yielding interest income – are taxed on their nominal return. Others – like company shares – are taxed on something much closer to their real return, thanks to the indexation of Capital Gains Tax (see box on page 35).

---

graphs which follow, with the different assets listed in approximate order of importance, the percentage after each heading giving the share of personal wealth held in each form at the end of 1986.[6] Figure 12a shows how the main components of personal wealth grew in real terms between the end of 1957 and the end of 1986.[7]

FIGURE 12a

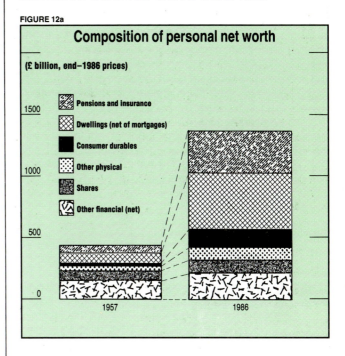

Composition of personal net worth

(£ billion, end–1986 prices)

- Pensions and insurance
- Dwellings (net of mortgages)
- Consumer durables
- Other physical
- Shares
- Other financial (net)

1500
1000
500
0

1957   1986

Owner occupied dwellings (34%, net of mortgages)

The return to owning one's own house comes in two forms: the value of living in it (the 'imputed rent') and the capital gain as its value increases. There used to be a tax (under 'Schedule A' of the Income Tax system) on imputed rents, but this was abolished in 1963. When Capital Gains Tax was introduced in 1965, owner-occupiers' 'principal private residences' were exempted. Meanwhile, the interest on up to £30,000 of a mortgage receives tax relief, reducing the net cost of borrowing by a quarter for most mortgagors. The combination of all of these features has been a key factor in Britain's very high level of owner occupation. Until now, owning a larger house has resulted in a higher rates bill, so that rates have been, at least in part, a tax on housing. The advent of the Poll Tax will remove this remaining offset to the tax advantages of housing.

Pension funds (about 14%)

Contributing to a pension fund so as to receive a pension later on can be thought of as a form of saving, and the assets held by a pension fund can be thought of as part of people's accumulated wealth. The tax treatment is again very favourable. First, contributions into a pension scheme are made out of pre-tax income. A basic rate taxpayer only has to give up £75 of post-tax income in order to have contributed £100 into a pension scheme. Against this, when regular pensions are paid out, they are fully taxable, *including* what amounts to the return of the capital originally paid in (in contrast to, say, withdrawing one's savings from a building society, where the capital is, of course, tax-free). If this was all there was to it, the advantage of tax relief on contributions would be cancelled out for most people: the £100 originally saved would be reduced to £75 again. The true advantage would then be that once invested, the interest, dividends and capital gains received by the pension fund are all tax-free. However, up to a quarter of one's pension rights can be paid out as a tax-free lump sum (limited to £150,000 for those joining pension schemes after March 1987) thus escaping the process of being scaled back down again. This is a very valuable concession indeed.

Building society and bank deposits (14%, including current accounts)

The interest paid by banks and building societies is fully taxable, with no allowance for the fact that part of the interest represents compensation for inflation rather than real income (see box on previous page). The interest paid out is deemed to be net of tax at the basic rate (higher rate taxpayers have to pay extra later on). What the institutions are charged is not, however, tax at the basic rate, but at a special **composite rate.** This rate (23.25% in 1988-89) is a weighted average of the zero rate which would otherwise be paid by non-taxpayers and the basic rate (currently 25%). This arrangement means that the correct *total* of tax is collected, but part of it from the 'wrong' people, as non-taxpayers cannot reclaim the tax which has been charged at source.

Life insurance (about 10%)

The major return from taking out life insurance is usually not, in fact, the value of the payments which would be made in the event of death, but the lump sum which is paid out at the end of the insurance contract – life insurance premiums are, in effect, a form of saving and the assets of the insurance funds are, largely, a form of personal wealth. As far as the income of the funds is concerned, dividends are taxed at the basic rate, while interest is taxed at 35%. Insurance companies also receive very generous allowances for deducting expenses. The Inland Revenue recently calculated that, if life insurance was taxed in the same way as unit trusts, the tax collected on their investment income in 1986 would have been *twice* the £700–800 million actually collected.[8] Capital gains are taxed at a special 30% rate, but the insurance companies have a wide range of options open to them to minimise or defer their liabilities. As the final payment is tax-free, these arrangements already offer advantages for higher rate taxpayers. For those who took out contracts before 1984 there is the added bonus of **Life Assurance Premium Relief,** under which the Government pays 12.5% of the premiums (a subsidy at half the basic rate for obscure historical reasons). In 1984 this concession was withdrawn for *new* contracts, one of the most important steps towards broadening the tax base made in recent years.

Consumer durables (9%)

Like houses, the return on owning durables like cars and washing machines comes from the value of using them without having to hire them or pay money to a laundrette. This return is, of course, untaxed.

Shares and unit trusts (8%)

Dividends on shares are taxed at the recipient's marginal tax rate. In the case of UK companies, dividends are paid net of the basic rate of tax; higher rate taxpayers have to pay more, while non-taxpayers can reclaim the 'tax credit' (see Section 19 for the way in which this is done through the 'imputation' system of Corporation Tax). A major part of the return on shares comes as capital gains, which are favourably treated relative to cash incomes, in particular through the generous annual exemption and the indexation allowance (see box opposite). There are special arrangements for taxing capital gains received by unit trusts, giving them further advantages.

Land and other buildings (6%)

Rents from land and commercial property are taxable, as are capital gains on it, but numerous concessions to agriculture and forestry erode the tax collected from land (especially inheritance and capital gains taxes).

Money and current bank accounts (about 3%)

These yield their returns in the form of the convenience of being able to spend them immediately – 'liquidity'– and in the services which banks provide free to their customers. This is another example of an untaxed return 'in kind'.

Gilts and other interest-bearing assets (3%)

The nominal interest paid on these is fully taxable, but any capital gain – for instance, because of a fall in interest rates – is tax-free. As a corollary, investors cannot use changes in gilt prices to create 'capital losses' and reduce their other Capital Gains Tax liabilities.

National Savings (2%)

Various forms of National Savings offer 'tax-free' returns, attractive to non-taxpayers (who would otherwise suffer the composite rate, for instance). The tax-free status means that the interest rate paid can be lower than it would be otherwise, while remaining competitive with the *post tax* return which basic rate taxpayers would receive from building societies or banks. The Government can therefore cream off most of the tax advantage for itself rather than for the saver (except for higher rate taxpayers who, once again, benefit most from tax concessions aimed at the 'small saver').

Taxation of investment income: a league table

The descriptions in this section should have explained the discrepancy between the value of personal wealth and the return on it which is taxed: nearly two-thirds of it is in forms which are effectively tax-free. Indeed, much of it is in forms which are *better than* tax-free: the tax system *adds* to their return. Putting together the effects of the treatment described above, one can obtain the following league table for the tax-conscious investor.

Much better than tax-free	Better than tax-free	Effectively tax-free	Taxed on real return	Taxed on nominal return
Share option schemes	Pension contributions	Houses owned outright	Shares and unit trusts	Building society and
Business Expansion		Consumer durables	*(more favourable if*	bank deposits *(at*
Scheme		Personal Equity Plans	*mostly capital gains)*	*composite rate)*
Pre-1984 life insurance		National Savings	Post-1984 life insurance	Gilts and other bonds
contracts		Forestry	*(more favourable for*	held directly.
Houses with mortgages		Money and current	*higher rate taxpayers*	
		accounts	*and if large deductions*	
			for expenses used).	

How Capital Gains Tax (CGT) works

If someone sells an asset like shares in a company for more than they paid for them, they 'realise' a capital gain. Since 1965, there has been a separate **Capital Gains Tax** on such gains. Tax is now only charged on the gain which accrues over and above inflation – there is an **indexation allowance** so that only the *real* gain is taxed. Gains which accrued before 1982 (that is, price rises which happened before then) are no longer subject to tax.

Until 1988, CGT was levied at a flat rate of 30%, but it is now at 25% or 40% depending on an individual's Income Tax rate. This linkage is a major step towards making the British tax system something much closer to a 'Comprehensive Income Tax' (see Section 13), although it is weakened by the fact that up to £5,000 of real gains can be realised each year tax-free.

Taxing capital gains is inevitably difficult. Taxing them when they actually accrue is generally ruled out – there is no cash flow with which to pay a tax bill. Tax is therefore levied on **'realisation'**, when the asset is sold. But this means that the payment of tax can be put off – deferred – for several years, reducing the value of the payment.

On top of this problem with any attempt to tax capital gains, the generous allowances in the current British system make CGT a worry only to the very wealthy or those unlucky enough to have to sell up and realise all of their gains in the same year. For instance, someone could own shares worth £100,000, increasing in value at 10% a year, but avoid any CGT liability: even if the £10,000 gain was realised each year, £5,000 could be set against the indexation allowance (if inflation was 5%) and the other £5,000 would be covered by the annual tax-free amount.

As an added twist to this, when independent taxation of husband and wife is introduced in 1990, their capital gains will also be taxed separately, with each entitled to £5,000 tax-free. But transfers between husband and wife will remain free of CGT. There will thus be nothing to stop one partner who would otherwise face a CGT bill passing assets to the other who would then realise the gain – with another £5,000 tax-free (and with any tax actually payable charged at 25% if they pay Income Tax at the basic rate, rather than 40%).

Capital Gains Tax (like Inheritance Tax) looks as if it might go the way of the dog licence: its revenue yield may eventually become so low compared with the hassle involved in calculating and collecting it that it will be 'obvious' that it should be abolished. This would not only be inequitable – why should those benefiting from large capital gains escape tax while those earning £100 per week pay it? – but would also further undermine the rest of the Income Tax system. One of the main activities of the tax avoidance industry is the creation of devices which turn what would otherwise be 'income' into much more lightly taxed 'capital gains'.[9] The outright abolition of CGT would make this problem far worse.

Miscellaneous

There are a number of other schemes which, while not very large in aggregate revenue cost, offer very large tax advantages to those with high incomes and good accountants. The **Business Expansion Scheme** is a device under which a higher rate taxpayer can give up what would have been £60 of post-tax income in order to buy £100 worth of shares, with the ability to sell them in 5 years' time without any tax due (except on the dividends received in the meantime). **Personal Equity Plans** allow people to invest up to £3,000 a year in shares which then yield tax-free dividends and capital gains (providing that the plan runs for at least a year). **Share option schemes** are a device under which employees and – especially – managers are given the right to buy a company's shares at a fixed price in the future whatever the actual price. This one-way bet amounts in most cases to a way of giving tax-free pay. Tax concessions to new investment in **forestry** were withdrawn in the 1988 Budget, but at the same time the return on forestry was made tax-free, so that those who reduced their pre-1988 tax bills by destroying ('investing in') irreplaceable parts of the Scottish wilderness will not now have to pay any tax when they receive income from it. **Personal pension schemes** not only receive the normal pension concessions, but an extra 2% addition to contributions for the 5 years from 1988. **Trusts** offer a legally complicated home for large fortunes which both avoids Inheritance Tax and reduces the tax charged on investment income.

Effects of variation of treatment

One obvious effect of this variation of treatment is that people hold as much of their wealth as possible in assets at the top of the league. As Figure 12a shows, the components of personal wealth which have grown most rapidly are rights in pension funds and insurance companies and owner occupied dwellings (shown net of mortgages). Direct share-holding and interest-bearing assets have hardly grown at all.

What has happened is a change in the channels of ownership. Pension funds rather than individuals now own most gilts (government bonds): this is much more **tax efficient.** Between 1957 and 1981, the proportion of UK company shares held directly by individuals rather than institutions fell from 66% to 28%[10] Rather than saving in a bank and renting a house (as happens in many other countries), anyone who can afford it becomes an owner occupier. Negotiating a good pension may be more important for many people than arguing for an equivalent pay rise.

Investors will choose to put their money into the assets which they think will offer them the best return (allowing for their attitude to any risk involved). Obviously the pre-tax return will be very important in this decision, but so will the tax treatment of that return. A further, less obvious, effect of the situation described above is that the assets with the best treatment tend to be those open to people with access to the most sophisticated advice and investing on a large enough scale for the 'transactions costs' (like stockbrokers' fees) to be worthwhile. The worst treated are those like bank and building society accounts which are most readily available to the small saver. This means that not only is the revenue potential of taxing investment income limited, but it is also less progressive than it could be if, for instance, all assets were fully taxed on their real returns.

Having said all this, it is crucial to recognise the phenomenon of **capitalisation:** the price of an asset may be increased by the fact that it benefits from a tax concession. Those buying it at that higher price are not any better off than they would have been without the tax concessions but with a lower purchase price. The classic example of this is owner occupied housing: if it was not for mortgage tax relief, new buyers would not be able to afford such large mortgages. They would therefore be able to offer less, and house prices as a whole would be lower. Withdrawing the concession overnight would hit recent buyers in two ways: their monthly payments would rise *and* the value of their house could well fall. Another example is the level of interest rates: these will be affected by the whole chain of taxation, from the tax deductibility of interest payments by companies against Corporation Tax through to the tax-free status of a pension fund receiving the interest or the composite rate paid by a bank depositor.

13. Fundamental reforms to the taxation of investment income

As the previous section has shown, the current system for taxing investment income is a mess: the returns on different forms of investment are taxed in widely different ways. This creates several problems. First, there is the *equity* problem already noted: those with their savings in one form will be more lightly taxed than those with theirs in another. This is certainly a problem of **horizontal equity:** people in similar circumstances are not being treated equally. It may also violate **vertical equity** if those with

higher incomes can exploit complicated savings schemes with tax advantages but which are not easily open to ordinary savers.

There are two further results of the situation. The tax system will encourage economic activity to take particular forms not because they would offer the best returns in its absence, but because they have the most favourable tax treatment: they are **tax privileged.** This will certainly erode the tax base, reducing revenues (and so increasing the tax rate on other activities) and may well also damage the operation of the economy.

Some discrimination between different kinds of activity could, of course, be desirable: taxation can be a useful tool with which the government can correct the failures of the market to take account of wider considerations than immediate private interests. Many of the concessions to particular forms of saving originated in a desire to encourage people to save more, particularly for the long term, but it is difficult to imagine that anyone starting from scratch would have designed the system just described. A few concessions to particular savings instruments may be

A Comprehensive Income Tax

Under a Comprehensive Income Tax (CIT), an attempt would be made to tax all forms of income equally, whether earnings in cash, fringe benefits provided by employers, interest income, dividends, capital gains or 'imputed returns' (like the value to owner occupiers of living in their own house). Holding assets indirectly through institutions like pension funds would not affect eventual tax liability. The taxation of benefits in kind like fringe benefits or imputed rents presents equivalent advantages and difficulties under either a CIT or an ET and so is not discussed further in the comparison below.

Two forms of CIT can be imagined, differing in their reaction to inflation. Under a 'nominal-based' CIT, the full return on investments would be taxed, with no allowance for the component of interest or capital gains which reflected inflation. As it is hard to justify in principle why more tax should be taken from investors simply because the rate of inflation has increased, the debate has concentrated – as will this discussion – on a 'real'-based CIT, with only the real return on investments taxable.

Advantages of a CIT

■ All incomes would be treated equally. There would be no distinction between earned and investment incomes or between incomes in cash or in kind. This can be argued to be much fairer in terms of horizontal equity – like would be treated in the same way as like. It would also eliminate the tax incentives which encourage people to save in one form rather than another.

■ The **tax base** – the total amount subject to tax – would be large (certainly larger than under an ET). The same amount of revenue could therefore be raised with lower tax *rates,* reducing the problems caused through any disincentive effects of taxation on earnings.

■ Because investment income would be fully taxable with no allowance for saving, a CIT would *for any given structure of tax rates* be more progressive than one incorporating savings allowances such as an ET (the structure of tax rates could, however, be changed – for instance, by having higher top tax rates in an ET – to make the two equivalent).

■ As many aspects of existing tax systems are an attempt to tax income rather than expenditure, some transitional prob-

lems would be avoided and relations with other countries would be relatively straightforward.

Problems with a CIT

■ It is extremely difficult to tax capital gains as effectively as cash incomes. The 1988 Budget made the important step of taxing capital gains at Income Tax rates, but true equivalence would require tax to be levied as soon as gains *accrued,* rather than later on when they were realised. But this means asking for a cash payment from people who have none to hand. If tax is charged on *realisation,* the tax rate charged has to be increased to remove the advantage of the delay. A formula could achieve this, but it would not be straightforward.[1] In addition, taxing capital gains on realisation has a 'lock-in' effect: people are encouraged to stick to their existing assets rather than to sell them – for instance, to move house.

■ Making an allowance for inflation within a CIT would be complicated. Such an allowance is already given in calculating Capital Gains Tax, but at some administrative cost. Coping with the much larger number of people with interest income would be much more difficult. Furthermore, in order to prevent tax avoidance, it would be necessary to ensure that when an allowance was given for inflation in taxing interest *receipts,* those paying the interest (say, companies or mortgagors) were only able to deduct their *real* interest *payments.*[2]

■ Coping with investment through the medium of institutions like pension funds or insurance companies is not easy. The tax levied on them would have to reflect the tax rates of all of those on whose behalf they operated. Strictly speaking, for instance, pension funds would have to be divided up into sections reflecting the various tax rates of their contributors at each moment.

■ The existing Income Tax base is not as close to a CIT as some think: pension fund taxation is much closer to an Expenditure Tax treatment, for instance. Unravelling this would be an administrative nightmare which would last a generation.

■ It is argued by some that income tax involves a 'double taxation of savings'. If someone earns and saves they will be taxed both on their earnings and on the return on their savings. Someone spending immediately is only taxed once. Certainly, any tax on investment income lowers the return on saving, which may discourage saving for some.

effective: many concessions competing with one another will have much more confused effects.

An important feature of the system as it is now is that **inflation** affects different forms of saving in different ways. In some cases – with a tax-free return or benefiting from the indexation of capital gains – taxation will be largely unaffected by inflation. In others – where the nominal return is taxed – tax will greatly increase as inflation rises; in some circumstances, the tax charged can exceed the real pre-tax return, an **effective** tax rate of over 100%. Savings decisions become even more of a gamble on the future inflation rate than they would have been anyway.

Faced with this, many economists have called for a **neutral** tax system,[3] that is, one in which the returns on different kinds of savings or investments are treated equally. Business and personal savings decisions would then be taken on their own merits, not with an eye to tax consequences; there would be what has been called a 'level playing field'. There would also be less scope for the escape of investment income into lightly taxed forms. For once, equity, efficiency and revenue-raising considerations all seem to point in the same direction.

The debate on such reforms has until recently been dominated by the choice between two 'ideal types' of taxation system: a **Comprehensive Income Tax** (CIT) or an **Expenditure Tax** (ET). These are described in the boxes, and have been discussed at length in the tax reform debates of many countries. In terms of practical policy-making, however, neither type has made much headway. CIT proposals have foundered on the administrative problems of taxing income in kind and capital gains effectively

and of allowing for inflation. ET proposals have been rejected on the basis of their negative effect on the government's cash flow, together with worries about progressivity and interactions with the rest of the tax system (especially company tax) and the difficulties which might emerge for one country which had introduced an ET while the rest of the world kept a more traditional system.

The theoretical debate has therefore shifted.[4] Actual systems have evolved as **hybrid income taxes,** with some parts looking like an income tax, while others look like an expenditure tax. In the British system, pensions are taxed on a basis quite close to an expenditure tax, while share ownership is taxed on a basis closer to a tax on real income. Having accepted that the system will be a hybrid, the question then becomes one of how to design it so that it is a good hybrid rather than a bad hybrid. This is explored in Section 14.

An Expenditure Tax

Under an Expenditure Tax (ET), the tax base would be the total of someone's income and their net *dis-saving* (the amount they spend out of their savings). By definition this would equal the amount spent each year. It would not be necessary to add all this up – tax would be calculated starting from income in the normal way but adding in any dis-saving and subtracting any saving. This is, for instance, quite close to the way in which pension funds are taxed at present: contributions (saving) are tax deductible while the pensions paid out (dis-saving) are fully taxable. Note that the tax could be charged according to a progressive rate schedule in the same way as the existing income tax – it would not have to be a flat-rate tax.

Advantages of an ET

■ Like a pure CIT, an ET would not distort the choice between different forms of saving. Tax would be based on what was eventually spent, not on the way in which the return appeared.

■ A key feature of an ET is that tax is only levied when cash is withdrawn from savings and spent. This sidesteps problems relating to the treatment of institutional saving, of capital gains and of allowing for inflation. None of the problems inherent in the way an income tax would deal with these problems arises.

■ As much existing saving (like pensions) is treated in a way which is quite close to ET treatment, the transition might be relatively straightforward.

■ An ET avoids the 'double taxation of savings' and may raise the savings rate and possibly, therefore, the rate of

growth. It has been described as a tax on what people take out of the economy rather than what they put into it.

■ Depending on how the transition to an ET is accomplished, in particular, how existing wealth and inheritance were treated, it could offer a way of taxing those who spent out of their inherited wealth: this could count as dis-saving and would therefore be taxable.

Problems of an ET

■ By making all saving tax-deductible an ET would reduce the size of the tax base (certainly compared with a CIT); in particular, those on higher incomes who tend to save more would see their immediate tax bills fall. To make up the government's cash flow, tax rates as a whole would have to be higher. To maintain progressivity, tax rates on people with higher incomes (who are able to save more of their incomes) would have to be raised more than others.

■ It would be difficult to run a personal ET at the same time as basing company taxation on income-related measures of profit. To be compatible, company taxation would have to be on a 'cash-flow' basis.[5]

■ Financial relations with countries maintaining an income base for their tax systems would become more complicated. There would be a danger that people would save here – benefiting from the tax deductibility of saving – and then move abroad – avoiding the tax on dis-saving. Taking assets abroad would have to be taxed as 'dis-saving' to avoid this.

■ On administrative grounds a distinction would have to be made between 'registered assets', the purchase of which would count as saving (such as a house), and 'unregistered assets' whose purchase would count as consumption (such as paintings). An actual ET would not be free of the 'barnacles' of special treatment which have already attached themselves to the income tax system.

14. Reforms within a hybrid tax system

One feature evident from the reviews of the current taxation of investment income in Section 12 and of the 'ideal types' of a Comprehensive Income Tax (CIT) or an Expenditure Tax (ET) in Section 13 is that many assets are currently outside the range between the two: their treatment is so favourable or so unfavourable that proponents of either a CIT or of an ET would agree on the direction of change.

Some assets are treated in a way which not only makes the return on them tax free (which is roughly equivalent to ET treatment), but the tax system actually *adds* to their return. These include the **Business Expansion Scheme** (with a revenue cost of £80 million in 1987–88)[1] and **share option schemes** (£200 million). Recouping revenue by abolishing these would not present enormous problems.

Removing the tax free status of **lump sums** paid to pensioners (with a revenue cost of £1,200 million in 1987–88) would be more problematic. Removing it overnight would create inequity between those pensioners retiring before the date and those retiring just after it. Phasing it out rapidly might encourage early retirement just to take advantage of it before it went. A long period would be required — say 10 years — during which the current £150,000 limit on lump sums was first applied to everyone (not just those newly entering pension schemes after March 1987, which is the current position) and then steadily reduced. As many pensioners would not then choose to 'commute' their pension into a lump sum, the revenue gain would build up over a rather longer period.

Similarly, the remaining **Life Assurance Premium Relief** (£520 million) could be phased out, say with the rate of relief reduced from 12.5% to zero over 5 years during which the revenue gain would build up. The overall treatment of life insurance – particularly the generous allowances for expenses – could also be tightened up, with a potential yield of £700-800 million at 1986 prices – see Section 12.

A more complicated issue is that much of **mortgage interest tax relief** (£4,750 million) would not be payable under a CIT (*real* interest payments *would* be tax deductible under a pure CIT, and not just for house purchase) or would be offset by later tax liabilities in the case of an ET. Here there are substantial problems both from capitalisation (see Section 12) in higher house prices and from the treatment of interest *receipts* elsewhere in the system. The most straightforward reform would be to remove higher rate relief (which is less likely to have been capitalised than basic rate relief) so that all relief was given at the same rate. Once this had been done, the relief could be redesignated as an interest rate subsidy (for instance of 3%, if the starting point was relief at 25% on interest rates of 12%). This could then come within normal public spending controls.

The assets more heavily taxed now than under either a real-based CIT or an ET are those paying **nominal interest** (such as bank or building society accounts). Moving towards either system would imply at least that the component of interest payments just reflecting inflation would not be taxed.[2] However, this would leave nominal interest payments tax *deductible* for mortgagors and businesses, while only real receipts were taxed. This could create a machine for tax avoidance (known in Latin America as the **'bicycle'** — tax is saved each time the money goes round). A partial solution would be to allow banks and building societies to offer indexed accounts (like 'granny bonds') on which only the real interest received would be taxable, *but* only to the extent that such accounts were matched by indexed loans or mortgages (on which only the real interest would be tax deductible).[3]

Moves towards a more comprehensive income base for taxation

The tax base could be broadened and moved further in the direction of a CIT by removing or reducing various Income Tax exemptions and by increasing the bite of Capital Gains Tax (for instance through reducing the extremely generous £5,000 annual allowance for tax-free real capital gains and by adjusting the rate of tax charged to offset the advantage of taxation on realisation rather than accrual).

The biggest item here is the tax-free status of pension fund income (costing £4.1 billion in 1987–88).[4] The key issue is trying to work out what the incidence of removing this concession would be. Many pension funds have very strong balance sheets at present, and probably have more assets than they need to meet their future pension liabilities. A tax on them might cream off these 'surpluses' without forcing the funds to demand higher contributions or to cut pensions promised for the future. In some ways, this would be what is usually thought to be impossible — a 'no loser' tax increase (the losers would actually be whoever will eventually benefit from the current surpluses — possibly the companies that contribute on their employees' behalf). The extent to which a tax on pension fund income could be imposed without resulting in higher contributions[5] or lower pensions would depend on the *rate* of tax imposed and the way in which it was phased in. A radical proposal that pension fund income should be taxed at the full basic rate (together with flat-rate taxation of investment income) is described in the box.

An investment income surcharge

A curiosity of the current tax system is the way in which the rate of tax charged on most earnings is higher than that charged on investment income as a result of National Insurance Contributions being levied on the former but not on the latter.[6] An obvious and progressive way of removing this would be to re-impose an equivalent to the old Investment

FIGURE 14a

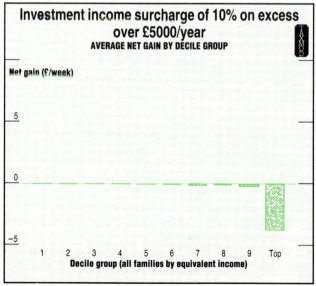

Investment income surcharge of 10% on excess over £5000/year
AVERAGE NET GAIN BY DECILE GROUP

Net gain (£/week)

Decile group (all families by equivalent income)

Flat-rate taxation of investment income

The current tax treatment of investment income results in discrimination between different ways of saving and of financing investment. Combined with the company tax system (see Section 19), it means that companies which raise capital by borrowing are favoured relative to those raising capital by issuing new shares (although much less so than when the company tax rate was higher) and that the best returns result when investments are made from retained profits (if the investor does not realise the resulting capital gain too quickly). Such effects would become much stronger if there was a return to higher top rates of tax.

Given that neither a full CIT nor an ET is on the practical agenda for reform, it has been suggested that these problems could be resolved by separating the taxation of investment income from earnings altogether and taxing it at a flat rate. For instance, one suggestion[7] is that interest should be taxed at the 25% basic rate (with the composite rate raised to the same level) and the tax paid at source on dividends could become the final payment. Income tax allowances would no longer be applied against investment income, but nor would the higher rate be charged on it (there would be no investment income surcharge within such a system). The income and capital gains of institutions like pension funds would also be taxed at the same rate (but with the tax phased in over, say, 10 years).

Not only would this achieve a high degree of 'neutrality' between different sources of investment finance (although this would not be perfect), but it would also solve two problems raised in earlier sections. First, tax could easily be levied at source, removing the administrative problems which otherwise arise with a graduated tax structure of the kind described in Section 5: the graduation would only apply to earned income (taxed via PAYE). Second, if investment income was taxed at a flat rate with no allowance, none of the problems connected with introducing independent taxation of husband and wife would arise: there would be no scope for tax avoidance by transferring assets from one partner to the other.

A problem with this kind of proposal in the context of shifting the tax system in a more progressive direction is shown in Figure 14b. At a 25% tax rate there would be a net revenue cost compared with current arrangements of £390 million (before allowing for the substantial revenue from taxing pension funds or for changes to capital gains taxation). Despite this, nearly 30% of families would lose, mostly from the small rise in the composite rate from 23.5% to 25% and from the loss of the ability to set investment income against tax allowances. A small number at the top would gain from the reduction in the tax on their investments from 40% to 25%. Such effects could, of course, be counteracted by other progressive elements within an overall package of tax reform; but they would make it more difficult to achieve a given degree of redistribution.

Within the framework of this argument, an equally strong case could be made that the flat rate of tax on investment income should equal the Corporation Tax rate — 35% — rather than the basic Income Tax rate.[8] If tax was imposed at 35%, there would be a revenue gain for the government of nearly £2 billion (compared with the 25% case), and most of this would be in the top half of the income distribution, making it a much more progressive way of raising revenue than that illustrated in Figure 14b.

The effects of flat-rate taxation of investment income would be rather different if the separate taxation system to be introduced in 1990 was already in place. The revenue yield from a given rate of tax would be higher, but, by the same token, more families would be affected.[9]

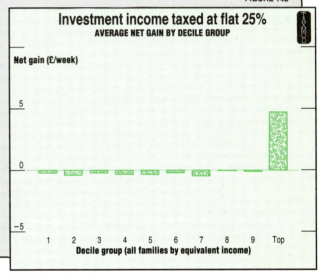

FIGURE 14b

Investment income taxed at flat 25%
AVERAGE NET GAIN BY DECILE GROUP

Net gain (£/week)

Decile group (all families by equivalent income)

Income Surcharge at a rate equal to the main National Insurance Contribution rate (an alternative, of integrating Income Tax and National Insurance Contributions is discussed in Section 7).

Figure 14a shows the distributional effects of imposing a 10% surcharge on investment income in excess of £5,000 a year (within the current joint taxation system for married couples). The total revenue raised amounts to £640 million, with less than 3% of all families losing, virtually all of whom are within the top 20% of the income distribution.

Imposing a surcharge on income above a lower threshold would raise more: if it was set at £2,605 (in line with the single income tax allowance), the revenue raised would be £900 million. However, the proportion of families losing would double to just over 5%, including some in the bottom half of the income distribution. Some pensioners with small amounts of income from investments rather than from an occupational pension scheme would be affected, and would object that the higher rate of tax was unfair compared with the treatment of occupational pensions.

The situation would be rather different if the surcharge was imposed within the 1990 system of separate taxation of investment income: as married couples would each have an allowance free of the surcharge, it would have to be set lower than £5,000 to raise the same revenue.

A problem with the imposition of an Investment Income Surcharge by itself is that it would increase the relative advantage of institutional investment, such as through pension funds, reinforcing the trends which have resulted in the shifts shown in Figure 12a. There might therefore be a strong argument that, even if pension fund income was not fully taxed (say at the basic rate), an equivalent of the surcharge should be imposed on pension funds at well. This would only raise a proportion of the full cost of the current exemption, but equally this might make it less contentious.

15. Taxing wealth and inheritance

The distribution of wealth is even more unequal than that of income as can be seen by comparing Figure 15a[1] for wealth, with Figure 2a for income.[2] In 1985, the top 5% of adults owned 40% of 'marketable' wealth (excluding pension rights, etc); by comparison, the top 5% in the income distribution received 11% of income.[3]

Some of the inequality of wealth holdings is due to the fact that people save up for retirement from their earnings. This **life cycle** pattern of savings inevitably means that wealth will not be distributed equally, particularly when one allows for the inequality of the distribution of earnings from which the savings are made. Nonetheless, the Royal Commission on the Distribution of Income and Wealth estimated that only a quarter of the share of the top 1% of wealth owners could be accounted for in this way — the rest being the result of inheritance or accumulated fortunes from sources other than earnings.[4]

Figure 15a shows figures from two sources for the shares of wealth of the top 5% and the top 1% of individuals. Atkinson, Gordon and Harrison (AGH) give consistent series between 1950 and 1981 (for Great Britain); the Inland Revenue (IR) series provide good estimates (for the UK) for more recent years, but are less consistent for earlier years.

The share of the top 1% halved between 1950 and 1975 but appears to have levelled out since then. The share of the rest of the top 5% (the top 2–5 percentiles) was virtually constant; indeed, their 20% share in 1985 was hardly changed from their 21% share in 1923![5]

FIGURE 15a

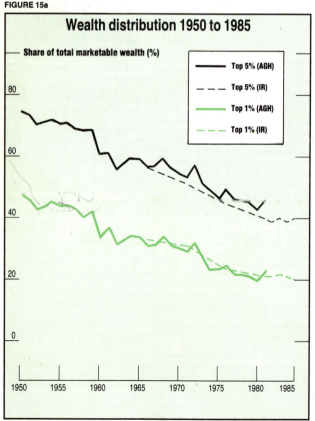

Wealth distribution 1950 to 1985

Meanwhile, the bottom half of the wealth distribution only owned 7% of marketable wealth in 1985 — £2,800 each, compared with an average of £400,000 each for the top 1%. Allowing for the value of occupational pension rights as well, the share of the bottom half rises to 8%–12%; including the value of state pension rights, the figure rises to 15%–19%.[6]

An annual wealth tax

A natural conclusion is that a tax on wealth could be aimed only at the very wealthy but still raise substantial revenue. There are other arguments in support of such a tax:

■ Wealth is more unequally distributed than income, making it a more progressive target for taxation.

■ Benefiting from wealth involves no sacrifice of leisure in the way that earning does — this can be said to raise the 'taxable capacity' of wealth owners and also means that there would be fewer disincentive problems.

■ Taxing the flow of *income* from wealth is difficult (see Sections 12–14). In particular, taxing the stock of wealth itself might avoid discrimination between assets.

Several European countries have, or have had, an annual tax on net wealth (after deducting debts) — including Austria, Denmark, France, Ireland, the Netherlands, Norway, Spain, Sweden and West Germany. Rates charged currently range up to 3% annually on the top slices of Swedish fortunes.[7] The experience of these countries has not, however, been encouraging. In particular, the idea of a comprehensive tax on wealth — avoiding the discrimination when the income from wealth is taxed in different ways — has proved hard to implement. In all cases pension rights are exempted, as are most household goods. The valuations put on dwellings and small businesses are usually favourable (putting an accurate value on a small business would be a very difficult task, so estimates err on the low side). Thus two-thirds of total wealth is treated favourably — the *same* two-thirds from which income is treated favourably.[8]

A tax aimed at the top 1% of wealth owners at the end of 1985 might have had a threshold of £250,000. A rate of 1% on the excess of marketable wealth over this would raise about £650 million a year (if there were no exemptions). This would, however, be the result of some 430,000 positive assessments for tax.[9] The administrative problems are obvious the moment one compares this with a tax involving an equivalent amount of administration in making a tax assessment. Capital Transfer Tax (CTT) raised £530 million from the estates of those dying in 1983–84, on the basis of 23,000 positive assessments.[10] The administration of an annual wealth tax could thus plausibly be *20 times* as burdensome as that of CTT while raising a similar amount. A threshold as low as £250,000 would also have the owners of 'modest' London houses lobbying for concessions, exemptions and other erosions of the tax's base.

A higher rate of tax from a higher threshold could get round both problems. A tax at the top Swedish rate of 3% on the excess of fortunes over £1 million would hit a manageable 20,000 or so of wealth owners and would bring in £600 million *if* there was no avoidance and there were no concessions. But this assumption is, to say the least, implausible. Given the lack of exchange controls, how would overseas assets be identified? Would the tax be on individuals, and if so, how much avoidance would there be through the use of transfers within the family? How would small businesses be valued? What about trusts? The number of assessments might be the same as for CTT, but they would be much more difficult: millionaires can afford the very best in tax avoidance. As time went by, there would almost certainly be attrition of the tax base through the steady drip of concessions and the learning of avoidance techniques. The Irish wealth tax in the 1970s, raising a pathetic £5 million annually from 2,400 cases at a significant political cost, is a depressing example.[11]

Taxes on capital transfers

At the heart of the problem with a wealth tax is the cost of administration in relation to its yield. This is why taxing *transfers* of wealth — inheritances and gifts — is often seen as more attractive. If wealth changes hands every generation — say, every 25 years — a tax at 25% on transfer would raise as much as a 1% annual wealth tax. Not only would one only have to cope with 4% of the number of cases each year, but they would also be easier: those receiving transfers have an interest in establishing legal ownership, making the wealth easier to identify.

Historically taxes on transfers, particularly inheritance, of wealth have been more important in the tax structure than they are now. Eighty years ago **estate duty** accounted for nearly 20% of tax revenue (excluding customs duties). By 1974–75, its last year before replacement by CTT, estate duty was raising 1.06% of tax revenues. The share of its successor CTT had fallen to 0.63% in 1978–79 and to a lowest point of 0.46% in 1982–83. Since then there has been a recovery, and the latest in the line, **Inheritance Tax**, raised 0.68% of tax revenues in 1987–88.[12]

However, these figures mainly reflect changes in other taxes and fluctuations in the value of wealth. A better measure of the performance of these taxes is their annual yield as a percentage of the value of marketable personal wealth (excluding consumer durables). This fell from 0.42% in 1958–59 to 0.26% in 1972–73, 0.14% in 1977–78 and 0.11%

in 1986–87; in other words, the effective yield is a quarter of what it was 30 years ago.[14]

Estate duty was flawed in that gifts made more than 7 years before death escaped. CTT therefore included gifts which people made during their lifetime, rather than at death (albeit at a lower rate), blocking this loophole; but by exempting transfers between spouses it covered a much narrower base and revenues continued to fall. After reductions in its rates and increases in the threshold between 1980 and 1986, CTT was replaced by Inheritance Tax in 1986–87. Lifetime gifts are again exempted (unless within 7 years of death, in which case reduced rates of tax are imposed). From 1988–89 Inheritance Tax is levied at a flat rate of 40% on the excess of estates over £110,000.

The major beneficiaries of these concessions have been those inheriting the largest estates; the prospects of living off inherited wealth are now brighter than they have been for many years (see box). Those looking to pass on family fortunes may well judge that now is the moment to do it: provided that the donor survives until 1995, wealth can be passed between the generations without tax. If at some later stage it was decided that a more stringent tax on capital transfers should be imposed, these particular horses, yachts and share portfolios would already have bolted for a generation.

Taxing capital receipts

Reconstructing the taxation of capital transfers would therefore be slow, starting from an almost blank sheet. When a new tax was introduced, one could introduce an important change of principle to the system. Hitherto taxes have been **donor-based** — the amount of tax charged depends on the total amount of the estate left, irrespective of how many people it is left to and of their circumstances. An alternative is a **recipient-based** tax, under which the tax levied depends on the amount each beneficiary receives. Under one variant, a **Lifetime Accessions Tax**, tax is charged according to the accumulated amount someone has received in gifts and bequests over their lifetime (there are many other variants, designed to achieve particular refinements).[15]

Suppose everyone was entitled to £50,000 of bequests or gifts free of tax. A millionaire could pass all of his wealth to his son — in line with the tradition of 'primogeniture' — in which case at least £950,000 would be taxable. Alternatively, he could leave it to 20 people who had not so far received anything, and there would be no tax at all.

If the desire to avoid tax altogether like this was widespread, little revenue would be collected — but the depressing conclusion of this section is that looking for much revenue in this area is in any case a rather forlorn hope. However, wealth would gradually be spread more widely through the population. Of course, this would initially be within a narrow band of the friends and relations of the very rich, but the current wealth distribution has to be seen as the product of centuries of primogeniture. In the long run, the heirs of the heirs are dead, like the rest of us; by then, the effects of spreading wealth might be worthwhile.

The rentier's return

A measure of the combined effect of changes over the last 10 years in Income Tax on investment income, Capital Gains Tax and Inheritance Tax is given by considering what post-tax return a married man inheriting £1 million would receive under the current tax system and what he would have received under the equivalent of the 1978–79 tax system (adjusted in line with income growth in the way explained in Section 3). The example does not allow for any special tax avoidance measures; in reality tax bills could be much lower.

Under the adjusted 1978–79 system, just under £0.5 million would have been payable in Capital Transfer Tax. Assuming the balance was invested to yield a 5% (gross) dividend and a 5% annual capital gain, the net annual dividend after paying Income Tax and Investment Income Surcharge would have been £15,450 and the net annual capital gain after Capital Gains Tax would have been £17,810. This leaves a comfortable total of £33,260 clear of tax.

Under the actual 1988–89 system, Inheritance Tax would be £356,000, leaving £644,000 to invest. Assuming the same return, the dividend after tax would now be £23,850 and the net capital gain £30,340 (allowing a conservative 3.5% indexation allowance). The £54,190 total is 63% higher than under the old tax system — a gain worth more than £400 per week.

This kind of gain to those with substantial unearned incomes contrasts with the position shown in Figures 1a and 1b: for a single person on average earnings, the direct tax cuts since 1978–79 have added less than 4% to disposable income, *all* of which has been wiped out by increases in indirect taxes.[13]

16. Value Added Tax

Value Added Tax (VAT) is the most important of the indirect taxes, forecast to raise £26.2 billion, or 15% of all tax revenue in 1988–89.[1] It is charged at a rate of 15% on most goods and services, with the exception of items like food, fuel and rent (which tend to be more important in the spending of those with lower incomes). The way it works is described in the box.

At the moment, there are three categories of goods for VAT purposes: those which are **exempt**, those which are **zero-rated**, and those which are **standard-rated**. There used to be a fourth category of 'luxuries' (electrical goods, cameras and so on) taxed at 12.5% (and earlier at 25%). When the standard rate was raised from 8% to 15% in 1979, the luxury rate was absorbed into it.

The distinction between 'exempt' and 'zero-rated' goods is arcane but important. An exempt concern (such as financial, health and education providers) simply does not have anything to do with the 'VAT-man': it buys things in the same way as anyone else, with VAT included, but does not charge VAT on its products. A zero-rated business (selling food, books, railway tickets, clothing classified as being for children, etc) not only does not have to charge VAT on its sales, but it can also *reclaim* any VAT already charged on its inputs. The price of a zero-rated item therefore would not include any VAT at all, whereas an exempt item might include the VAT which had been charged on the supplier's inputs.

The progressivity of VAT

Indirect taxes are usually expected to be regressive because those on higher incomes save more of their incomes, and hence spend less on which to be taxed. This is not true in the case of VAT, however, because of the zero-rated items and the exemption of housing. These items are more important in the spending of those on low incomes, as can be seen from Figure 16a.[2] Note that the income groups are not the same as those used in other sections: the unit of analysis is the household, no allowance has been made for family composition, the measure is gross rather than net income and the sizes of the eight groups vary as shown in the table opposite. The proportion of spending liable to VAT rises from 41% for the lowest income group of 63% for the highest.

The progressive effect of zero-rating cancels out the regressive effect of higher income groups spending a smaller proportion of income, and makes the impact of VAT mildly progressive, as can be seen looking at Figure 17a in the next section. In 1985, VAT took 5.9% of the disposable income of the poorest fifth of households (ranked by original incomes), compared with 7.3% for the richest fifth and 7.4% for all households.[3]

This has two important implications. First, a shift of emphasis from a *more* progressive tax, like Income Tax, to VAT — as happened in 1979 — will be to the disadvantage of lower income households. Secondly, removal of the zero-rating of items like food would turn VAT from a mildly progressive tax to a regressive one. This possibility has now been put on the agenda by the European Commission.

The VAT base

In recent years there has been a slow erosion of the zero-rated items. Construction classed as 'improvement' is now standard rated, as 'repairs' already were, although building new houses is still zero-rated. Hot take-away food was brought into the VAT net in 1984 and the 1988 Budget dramatically extended VAT to crunchy cereal bars.

Rather more important than these policy measures have been the changes in consumption patterns which have come from rising incomes and changes in income distribution. For instance, in 1979, 17.8% of all household spending was on zero-rated foods, while by 1986 the proportion had fallen to 14.6%.[4] Without any government action, the VAT base now covers a greater proportion of spending — another way in which the tax burden has increased invisibly.

The European Commission's proposals[5]

As part of the move towards the 'completion of the internal market' in the European Community by 1992, the Commission in Brussels has proposed that the twelve member states should 'harmonise' their VAT structures and set rates which 'approximate' to one another. If implemented, this would have major implications for the UK. In particular, zero-rated items like food, fuel, water, books and passenger transport would have to pay at least 4% VAT while some items like children's clothing would have to pay at the full standard rate (15% in Britain).

The motivation for this proposal appears to be the following. If one country charges a low rate of VAT, it will be difficult for its neighbours to charge a higher rate without some of its citizens crossing the border to take advantage of the lower prices (normal exports pay VAT in the country where they are sold, so there is no problem for them). As border controls are removed this will become easier. It already happens to some extent — people from Belgium (standard VAT rate 19% in 1987) and France (18.6%) shop in Luxembourg (12%). In the same way, British day-trippers return from Calais weighed down with wine to save paying British excise duty.

FIGURE 16a

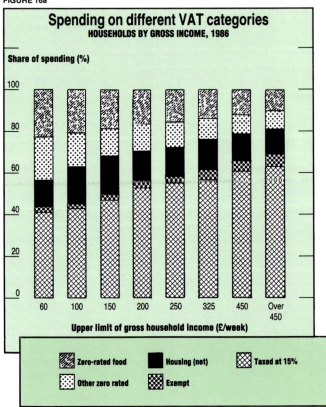

Spending on different VAT categories
HOUSEHOLDS BY GROSS INCOME, 1986

Share of spending (%)

Upper limit of gross household income (£/week)

Zero-rated food | Housing (net) | Taxed at 15%
Other zero rated | Exempt

How VAT works

Something that one buys in a shop has already, in whole or in part, been through a series of earlier transactions during which raw materials have been purchased, components sold to a manufacturer and the finished product passed first to a wholesaler and then to a retailer. At each of these stages, those involved in the commodity do something — either by physically changing it or by moving or marketing it — which enables them to charge a higher price than they paid for their inputs. Their labour 'adds value' to the product.

The intention of VAT is that tax should be collected at each stage in this process in proportion to the value added by that stage — hence its name. As a very simple example, consider what happens as a piece of crockery, say a mug, goes through this process:

STAGE 1: Someone extracts clay from the ground and sells it on to a pottery company. The price of the clay for one mug is 10 pence before tax, so the tax on the value added is 1.5 pence, which is sent to the government.

STAGE 2: The pottery company pays 10 pence for the clay and the 1.5 pence VAT (11.5 pence in total), and turns it into a mug which they sell to a retailer, adding 40 pence to its price. They therefore charge 50 pence plus 15% VAT, or 57.5p. The actual amount they send to the government is the difference between the 7.5 pence VAT due on their sales less the 1.5 pence they have already paid on their inputs, that is 6 pence.

STAGE 3: The retailer adds a mark-up of 50p, taking the pre-tax price to £1.00, or £1.15 including VAT. The net tax sent off at this point will be the 15 pence due on sales, less the 7.5 pence already paid on inputs — that is, 7.5 pence.

The total amount of tax collected by this process is 15 pence (1.5 pence plus 6 pence plus 7.5 pence). This is 15% of the £1 the mug would have cost without the tax, and the tax collected at each stage is in proportion to the value added at that stage (10 pence, 40 pence and 50 pence). This is achieved through the way in which tax is charged on each transaction, but with a credit for the tax already charged at earlier stages. If a credit was not given for the tax charged at earlier stages, the amount eventually collected would be larger the greater the number of stages there were, a process known as 'cascading' (which has undesirable effects on the way the economy is organised).

A simpler way of achieving the same result would be for the earlier — 'intermediate' — transactions to be free of tax, but simply to charge 15% on the retailer's full sale price. This is precisely how VAT's predecessor in Britain, purchase tax, worked and how 'retail sales taxes' still work in a number of countries such as the USA.

Worldwide, however, VAT is gradually supplanting sales taxes as the predominant form of indirect tax. This is because VAT has advantages in enforcement. Under a sales tax, transactions take place free of tax until the final stage, bringing a danger that goods may slip through to the consumer tax-free. In addition, although more complex to administer, collecting relatively small amounts from several people appears to be less open to evasion than leaving it all in the hands of a single person, the retailer. In Britain, the introduction of VAT had more to do with the fact that the rest of the European Community had introduced VAT to replace earlier taxes which suffered from cascading and as a way of catching services which had escaped purchase tax.

In order to prevent such cross-border shopping eroding their own tax bases, countries therefore have an interest in persuading their neighbours not to undercut their indirect tax rates. This seems to be the reason for the Commission's proposals (although it does not explain why it has also proposed a *maximum* to the rates of VAT which can be charged).

This may be a strong argument in the case of Luxembourg, with land borders with three other EC members. It is a much weaker argument when applied to the UK whose land border is with Ireland, the only other member state to zero-rate a wide range of items. Why should the two countries have to impose VAT on food simply to discourage cross-border shopping which would only take place because the other has been forced to do the same? True, it is possible to imagine that the French might flood through the Chunnel to buy zero-rated food in Dover supermarkets — but only by hypothesising a rapid change in the French opinion of British food.

While the argument for the Commission's proposals does not seem very strong, they would have significant distributional effects. The table shows, for the same groups of households as in Figure 16a, what would have been the effects in 1986 of making the minimum changes needed to comply (the figures do not allow for any resulting changes in spending patterns). On average, households would have paid an extra £2.05 per week in VAT, 1.1% of disposable incomes. The size of the cash losses would be smaller for those at the bottom than those at the top, but this loss would represent a much greater proportion of their incomes. The loss would be 2.3% of income at the bottom, falling to 0.7% at the top.

Effect of European Commission proposals for VAT (1986)[6]

Range of gross household income (£ per week)	Percentage of households	Additional tax (£ per week)	As percentage of disposable income
Under £60	Bottom 12%	0.99	2.3
£60–£100	Next 15%	1.40	1.8
£100–£150	Next 13%	1.75	1.6
£150–£200	Next 12%	1.98	1.3
£200–£250	Next 11%	2.12	1.1
£250–£325	Next 14%	2.36	1.0
£325–£450	Next 14%	2.71	0.9
Over £450	Top 10%	3.36	0.7
Average	All	2.05	1.1

If the proposals were implemented, they would generate extra government revenue. If this was used to cut progressive taxes like Income Tax, the net effect would benefit the top of the income distribution, but mean losses at the bottom. Alternatively, it is possible that the revenue could be used in a way which would counteract — or even more than counteract — the regressive effects shown in the table, for instance, by raising benefits and tax allowances.[7] However, even with this kind of package there would be a danger. In the short term, offsetting adjustments might indeed be made — but in the longer run, these might be absorbed into the normal process of keeping benefits and tax allowances up with inflation. Defending the progressivity of the tax system is a constant battle; the loss of zero-rating might mean conceding ground which would never be regained.

17. Drinking, driving and smoking

As well as VAT, levied equally on most spending (with the exceptions discussed in Section 16), there are indirect taxes on particular kinds of spending. These include rates (discussed in Section 18), the **Excise Duties** on tobacco, alcohol and petrol, **Vehicle Excise Duty, Car Tax** and **betting and gaming duties.**

The combined impact of all of the indirect taxes is shown in Figure 17a[1] in relation to *disposable* income (that is, after deducting Income Tax and National Insurance Contributions). Apart from the effects of saving, a 'neutral' indirect tax which affected the spending of all income groups equally would then represent a constant proportion of their disposable incomes (but the proportion of gross income would fall with rising income, because of direct taxes). The household groups are ranked on the basis of income before taxes and benefits (with no adjustment for household sizes). 'Intermediate' taxes paid by producers are excluded.

FIGURE 17a

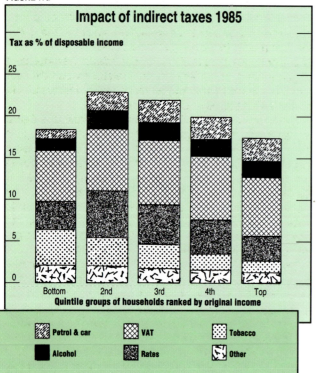

Overall, the impact is mixed. As a result of rate rebates and zero-rating for VAT, the proportion of disposable income taken from the poorest fifth (quintile group) of households, 18%, is less than the average. Above this they are regressive, the total falling from 23% of the disposable income of the second quintile group of households to 17% for the richest fifth.

What is also clear, however, are the great differences in the impact of the various taxes. Petrol and car taxes (including Vehicle Excise Duty) are mildly progressive (but see below), while VAT and taxes on alcohol take least from the bottom fifth but, apart from that, are roughly proportional.

The most striking feature is the regressive impact of rates (except for the effect of rebates at the bottom) and, in particular, of tobacco taxation. Tobacco taxation represents 4.3% of the disposable income of the poorest fifth, but only 1.3% for the richest fifth. The 'other' taxes are also regressive, mainly as a result of the flat-rate TV licence.

What the diagram does not show, of course, is the variation *within* the income groups. If the poorest fifth as a whole are spending 4.3% of their disposable income on tobacco taxes, the families within the group containing at least one smoker — rather less than half of them[2] — will be spending 9% of their disposable income on tobacco tax. There will be similar variations within other income groups.

Why tax particular goods?

There is a substantial theoretical literature on the extent to which it is useful to levy different rates of indirect taxes on particular goods.[3] One conclusion from this literature — the 'Ramsey rules' — is that economic behaviour will be least distorted if the heaviest taxes are levied on goods for which price changes have little effect on demand (those which are 'price inelastic').

This is not necessarily very helpful, as minimising economic distortion is only one aim; distributional aims also have to be met. If minimising economic distortion was the only aim of taxation, the logical outcome would be that all taxes would be replaced by a poll tax! The goods with the least response to price changes are likely to be the 'necessities' featuring prominently in the budgets of the poor, while the most price responsive may well be 'luxuries' consumed by the rich. Taking account of distributional objectives leaves no clear theoretical result.[3]

Looking at the list of goods subject to high rates of indirect taxes, one can discern a number of motivations:

■ They are a *soft target* — public objections to 'sin taxes' like those on drinking, smoking and gambling may be muted.

■ They are *luxuries* — taxing motoring, wine and spirits is a way of making indirect taxes less regressive.

■ They are intended to affect *behaviour* — increasing the price of activities like drinking and smoking, which have costs for the community, may discourage people from indulging in them.[4]

■ They are a form of *user charge* — tolls do not have to be paid to use the roads, so a tax on petrol is a way of charging motorists in proportion to the amount they drive (which makes the 'progressivity' of taxes on motoring more dubious — those on higher incomes pay more tax because they use the roads more).

■ They are a disguised *tariff* — taxing wine more heavily than beer used to be a way of giving a tax preference to home-produced goods.

As has often been observed elsewhere, these objectives can be in conflict. The 'soft target' argument implies that the aim is raising revenue, in which case it will be most effective when demand is not greatly affected by price; but the behavioural argument is based on the idea that demand *is* responsive.

Perhaps the greatest dilemma is presented by tobacco taxation. There are strong arguments for using taxation to encourage smokers to cut down, and research suggests that higher prices do have this effect (although it may not make much difference to *who* smokes, just to how often smokers light up[5]). But as Figure 17a shows, tax on tobacco is highly regressive — an example of what has been called 'the inequity of taxing iniquity'. In view of this, there may be a strong case for strengthening alternative ways of discouraging smoking — more effective health education and making the purchase of tobacco more difficult — rather than imposing such high taxes on people with low incomes.

The structure of Excise Duties

As a rule, Excise Duties are fixed as **specific amounts**, a cash amount for a given quantity. For instance, the excise duty on whisky works out at £4.73 a bottle (if it is of average strength) regardless of the retail price. Similarly, Vehicle Excise Duty is £100 a year for all private cars, regardless of their value. As an exception, the duty on tobacco has an **ad valorem** component, that is, part set as a proportion of the retail price. For instance, for cigarettes the duty (in 1988–89) is worked out as £30.61 per 1,000 cigarettes plus 21% of the retail price. Goods which carry duties also carry VAT, of course; note that VAT is calculated on the *total* of the pre-tax price and the duty.

The effects of the main duties in 1987 are illustrated in Figure 17b.[6] As a proportion of the pre-tax price (sometimes called 'factor cost'), tobacco is now the most heavily taxed. For instance, of the typical £1.52 retail price of a packet of 20 king size cigarettes in 1987, only 39 pence represented the pre-tax price; 74% of the price was tax of one kind or another. At the other end, 29 pence or 35% of a typical 82 pence price of a pint of beer in 1987 represented duty and VAT. The effect of specific duties is that the tax as a proportion of price *falls* for more expensive products. Only 20% of the price of a bottle of a rather nice claret retailing for £10 would, for instance, reflect tax, as opposed to 40% for the bottle of supermarket plonk shown in the diagram.

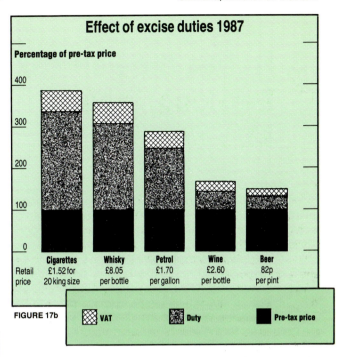

FIGURE 17b   VAT   Duty   Pre-tax price

Inflation and specific duties

One feature of the structure of excise duties is that it is not robust against inflation. Chancellors have to run hard against 'Budget hits drinkers and smokers' headlines just to stay in the same place because, left to themselves the cash amounts specified lose their real value. Between 1966 and 1978, for instance, the indirect tax on cigarettes lost 28% of its real value, that on petrol 26% and that on whisky 45%.[7]

Since then, there has been more awareness of the need to 'index' the duties for inflation each year. However, as the table shows, the picture has not been uniform. Looking at the taxes as a percentage of the pre-tax price (factor cost), only that on whisky (and other spirits) has fallen, while the tax on petrol has risen dramatically. Alternatively, looking at the real value of the tax on typical products in 1978 (adjusted by the RPI) compared with those in 1987, the duties break into two groups. Those on cigarettes, beer and petrol have been increased faster than inflation, rising by about 40% in real terms, while those on wine and spirits have continued to lag behind, falling by nearly 20% since 1978.

Taxes on Alcohol, Tobacco and Petrol 1978 to 1987[8]

	Tax as percentage of factor cost 1978	Tax as percentage of factor cost 1987	Tax in 1987 as percentage of tax in 1978 (at 1987 prices)
Whisky	364	255	81
Cigarettes	235	289	143
Petrol	76	183	132
Wine	54	66	80
Beer	44	54	143

The European Commission[9]

Part of the reason for the changes shown in the table has, of course, been pressure for 'harmonisation' with the rest of the European Community. Indeed, in 1984 the duty on wine was actually cut, after a ruling that the differential between wine and beer taxation in the UK constituted a hidden tariff.

As part of its proposals for completion of the internal market in 1992, the European Commission has proposed that excise duties should be set at the same rate throughout the Community (not even just 'approximated' as with VAT). This is because it wants all border controls on the movement of goods lifted, but differential duty rates between different members would be harder (but by no means impossible) to sustain without some kind of border control.

The good news for British drinkers and smokers is that, if implemented, these proposals would mean massive cuts in the duties on alcohol and a fall in those on tobacco (but not petrol). The Commission has proposed common duties which are a simple average of those applying at present in the member states. In 1986, this would have meant, for instance, a cut of nearly 90% in the duty on wine and up to 75% in that on beer. The proposals for tobacco would change the balance of specific and ad valorem components, leaving the retail price up to 10% lower than now.

These changes are so large that, if they were implemented, they would have significant effects on consumer behaviour. The volume of alcohol consumed would, on one estimate, rise by a third.[10] This would mean that the revenue loss to the Government would be moderated somewhat — there would be more alcohol sold on which to collect the lower tax. Allowing for such effects, it has been calculated that the net effect of these proposals, combined with those for VAT discussed in the previous section would be a small revenue gain for the Government.[11] Interestingly, the *progressive* effect of the proposed cut in tobacco tax is such that it would reverse the regressive effects of the VAT changes proposed by the Commission.

Revenue-raising and distributional effects are not the only considerations here, however, and there are other ways of achieving the same results. The effects on health of greater smoking and drinking and the wider social effects of anything like an increase of a third in the consumption of alcohol, present a strong argument against this kind of change unless accompanied by non-fiscal measures which would work in the other direction.

18. Rates, the Poll Tax and local income tax

Rates are forecast to raise £19 billion in 1988–89 — 11% of total tax revenues.[1] Unlike other taxes, they are controlled by local rather than central government (although the grant system and 'rate-capping' have meant that the central government now has a very strong influence over them).[2]

Rates can be divided into **domestic rates**, paid by households, and **non-domestic rates**, paid by businesses. The amount due is arrived at by multiplying together the property's **rateable value** and the local **rate poundage** — the tax rate set for the year by the local authority. Domestic rate poundages are slightly lower than non-domestic ones as a result of a central grant, **domestic rate relief**.

Rateable values are meant to reflect the rents which properties could command (net of maintenance and other costs). These change over time, so there ought to be regular revaluations to keep *relative* values in line with reality (the effects of general inflation can be counteracted by increases in the rate poundages charged). The last time this happened in England and Wales, however, was in 1973. The amounts now being paid thus depend on an estimate of what properties could have been rented out for 15 years ago! Subsequent revaluations have been cancelled, partly to save money, and partly for fear of the reaction if relative rateable values changed. When there was a revaluation in Scotland in 1985, the unhappiness of the losers was much more vociferously voiced than the gratitude of the gainers (illustrating a general pitfall of tax reform).

Because rateable values do not change from year to year, revenue does not automatically keep up with incomes or inflation: rates are not **buoyant**. Local authorities therefore have to keep increasing rate poundages each year, even if their spending is no higher in real terms.

Rates only pay for around half of local authority spending. The rest comes from central government **Rate Support Grant**. The most important part of this, **Block Grant**, depends on a complicated formula, set in part to give most to authorities with a high *need* to spend and those with low *resources* (in terms of the total rateable value of properties in the area). The current formula also punishes authorities which spend more than the Government thinks they should; they then have to charge much higher rate poundages.

This system is all going to change, with domestic rates being replaced by the **'Community Charge'** or **Poll Tax**, as it has become generally known (and as it will be described below). The box describes the other changes which will accompany this.

Principles of local taxation

Some qualities of a good local tax would be desirable for any tax. It should not damage the **efficiency** of the economy — although a single tax should not necessarily be looked at in isolation (one of the advantages of rates is that they partly make up for the otherwise favourable tax treatment of housing — it can also be argued that there is a need for a tax on property in its own right). It should be easy to **administer**, and should not be open to evasion or avoidance. It should

be **buoyant**, rising in line with prices or incomes (although one reason why rates are allocated to local government is because successive central governments have not wanted them to have a buoyant tax).

Other qualities relate to its local nature. It should be **locally variable**, so that authorities are free to make different choices on spending and tax levels. It should be **visible**, so that people are aware of the result of their voting decisions (again, central governments prefer to keep invisible taxes for themselves). Its impact should be on the same geographical area as is used to elect those setting local spending levels.

The extent to which it should be **progressive** is a matter of dispute. There are the usual distributional arguments for progressivity, but there is a danger that progressive local taxes may lead to the kind of flight of the affluent to low tax suburbs, leaving behind impoverished high tax cities that has been seen in the USA. Similarly, high taxes on businesses in poor areas may drive employment to low tax areas.

It has been suggested that to avoid this, the **'benefit principle'** should apply: local taxes should reflect the benefits people receive from local government, without any overall redistributive effect. Adding the *assumption* that those living in an area benefit equally from local services, this appears to justify a poll tax. However, there is little local choice on the level of 'statutory' services which local government provides on an 'agency' basis for central government. These general or 'spill-over' benefits are one of the reasons for central grants to local authorities. Secondly, particularly for non-statutory services, use is *not* equal between different people. Recent research[3] suggests that those on higher incomes use local services more than those on lower incomes; strict application of the benefit principle might favour rates rather than a poll tax, although neither exactly reflects the pattern of service use.

The second box assesses the different options for a local tax in the light of these requirements.

The Poll Tax package

Replacement of domestic rates by the Poll Tax or 'community charge' is only one of four linked measures being introduced into the whole system of local government finance:[4]

■ The **maximum rebate** for rates or the **Poll Tax** has already been cut from 100% to 80%. This is to stop people being 'insulated' from the effects of voting decisions through Housing Benefit covering all of any tax increases.

■ The **Poll Tax** will replace domestic rates from April 1989 in Scotland, and April 1990 in England and Wales. Instead of a 'transitional period' as originally envisaged, this will happen overnight.

■ Non-domestic rates will be replaced by a **Uniform Business Rate** (UBR). This will be charged on the rateable value of business premises as now, but at a fixed national rate. Revenue from the UBR will be pooled between local authorities in proportion to population.

■ The grant system will be changed so that each authority will receive **Revenue Support Grant** at a *fixed* level, regardless of its spending. Grant will be calculated so that each authority would be able to balance its books while charging the same level of Poll Tax, if they each spent at the level central government lays down as being necessary to provide a 'standard' level of service.

Local taxes – pros and cons

■ **Rates** have the great advantage that they are levied on something with a fixed location which is hard to hide. They score well in terms of low administration costs, difficulty of evasion and visibility. As a tax on housing, they balance some of the other aspects of the tax system although they do not reduce the relative advantages of owner-occupation against other tenures. They score poorly in terms of buoyancy and they also vary widely between localities, creating the need for significant 'equalisation' grants. Their link with ability to pay is weak: people with higher incomes *do* tend to have larger houses, but a special system of rebates (part of Housing Benefit) is needed to prevent rates from being unacceptably regressive.

■ **Local sales taxes** — such as a locally variable addition to the VAT rate — would be buoyant and would be related to spending as a measure of ability to pay. However, the 'cross-border shopping' problem (see Section 16) would be acute if there were variations between areas only a few miles across. People do not necessarily shop in the area in which they vote; variations in tax rates would make this worse. British local authorities simply cover too small an area for local sales taxes to be feasible.[5]

■ The **Poll Tax** will certainly be visible. Apart from that, it is hard to see any merits in it, unless one argues that use of local services is uniform and applies the 'benefit principle' (but see text). It will not be buoyant. It is less well related to ability to pay than rates and will continue to require a rebate system. It will, even according to the Government, cost twice as much to administer as rates (as there will be twice as many people paying it), and this has been widely criticised as an underestimate.[6] It will be hard to enforce on mobile parts of the community and may be widely evaded; the methods of control to try to prevent evasion raise major civil liberties issues.

■ A **Local Income Tax** (LIT) would mean that each local authority would set a tax rate to be applied to people's incomes. LIT scores best on ability to pay and buoyancy. Incomes also vary less between localities than rateable values, so less strain would be put on equalisation grants.[7] It would remove the need for a rebate system altogether. Its administration would probably require changes to the system for collecting national income tax;[8] some of these might be desirable in their own right, but they would have costs. It would be necessary to identify where people live, but this would not be necessary for those with very low incomes — precisely the groups which will be most difficult to identify in administering the Poll Tax. In many ways it is much easier to identify incomes than people. Administration would be easiest if an LIT applied to earnings only (although this raises an equity issue). If the rates of an LIT were high, they might have disincentive effects on labour supply (although the end of rate rebates would improve incentives by cutting away part of the poverty trap), and high LIT rates might also lead to the 'flight to the suburbs' problem described in the text.

The effects of the Poll Tax package

In the fourth edition of their standard text on the British Tax System 'brought up to date as of 1 January 1986', John Kay and Mervyn King wrote, 'a poll tax could not replace rates, unless levied at unimaginably high levels'.[9] In January 1986, the Government published its Green Paper, *Paying for Local Government*, which made that imaginative leap back to the fourteenth century (when an earlier attempt to introduce a poll tax led to the Peasants' Revolt).

Figure 18a, adapted from that Green Paper,[10] shows the effects (at 1984–85 tax and income levels) of the switch from rates to the Poll Tax *by itself*, that is, not of the other elements of the reform package outlined in the box (like the UBR or the new grant system), and assuming that the 80% maximum rebate was already in place. Even so, there are two effects happening at once. For households containing the same number of adults, there is a gain for those with high rateable values and a loss for those with low ones. This is regressive. At the same time, there is a gain for one-adult households compared with those with several adults. This is largely progressive — for instance, because the former group includes pensioners living by themselves — but is not enough to offset the first effect.

It is important to look at *equivalent* income here, because household composition is so important; looking at effects just in relation to total household income would be very misleading. However some care is needed in interpreting the diagram. The ranges of equivalent income shown do not contain equal numbers of households. The Green Paper does not say how many are in each range, but on the basis of the 1988–89 distribution shown in Figure 2d adjusted for income growth, only the top 10% of households will be in the ranges with equivalent income above £150 per week, where the gains occur. Essentially what Figure 18a shows is that there will be significant gains for the top 10%, but (to pay for it) a small overall loss for the rest of the population. There will, of course, be substantial shifts *within* the rest of the income distribution.

On top of these effects (and those of the 80% maximum rebate taken into account in Section 3), the UBR and the new grant system will cause major shifts of revenue between local authorities, and hence their taxpayers. These effects are complicated, as they start from the complex base of the existing grant system. This already redistributes resources from authorities with a high level of non-domestic rateable value per capita, to those with a low level, so the fact that this will happen directly under the UBR does not have major effects (*except* for a few authorities like the London Borough of Camden[11]).

The major effects come from the change in the grant system. First, authorities spending at the level laid down by the Department of the Environment (their 'Grant Related

FIGURE 18a

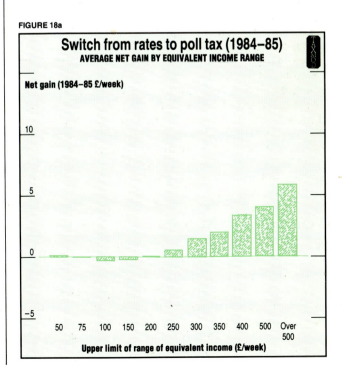

Switch from rates to poll tax (1984–85)
AVERAGE NET GAIN BY EQUIVALENT INCOME RANGE

Net gain (1984–85 £/week)

Upper limit of range of equivalent income (£/week)

Expenditure' GRE), will balance their books if they charge a standard Poll Tax, rather than a standard rate poundage as now. This shifts resources *from* areas with low domestic rateable values — like the North — *towards* those with high levels — like the South-East[12]. Secondly, some of the special arrangements designed to keep down London rate levels will disappear, reducing the amount of grant going to London.

The final effect is the way in which Poll Tax levels will be related to local authority spending. Figure 18b shows an example in which an authority spending an amount equal to its GRE, in this case £1,000 per adult, would charge a Poll Tax of £250. Half of its spending would be financed by Revenue Support Grant and a quarter by its share of the UBR. This is the middle column of the diagram. Any extra spending decided on by the local council would *all* have to be paid for through a higher Poll Tax. In this case, a 15% higher spending level would mean a Poll Tax of £400 — *60%* higher. Conversely, if spending was 15% below GRE, the Poll Tax would only be £100, 60% lower than the standard.

This heavy **gearing** between spending levels and the Poll Tax happens because the 'discretionary base' of local authorities will be so narrow under the new system: at least 75% of their revenue will come from sources outside their control. Part of the point of the new system is to discourage high spending levels by means of this gearing effect and through the knowledge that those worst hit will be those on the lowest incomes.[13] The aim of the system is that marginal spending changes are fully borne by Poll Tax payers.

In addition, it should be noted that the Department of the Environment assessment of the cost of a 'standard' level of service is not necessarily very accurate (and is also open to political manipulation). 'Mistakes' in the assessment will have the same effect on the Poll Tax as a change in spending: a 15% 'error' could mean a 60% increase in the local Poll Tax.

Putting all the effects together, Government figures suggest that the Poll Tax for two-adult households will be about 30% higher than current rate bills on average in the North, Yorkshire and Humberside, and 90% higher in Inner London, but 20% lower in the South-East outside London.[14] This will not happen immediately. There will be a system of 'safety nets' for the grants going to local authorities, which will mean that local tax levels will move towards the new levels over several years. It will be the mid-1990s before the full impact of the whole package will be clear.

Alternative reforms of local taxation

This short review leads to the following conclusions:

■ The Poll Tax is wholly unacceptable on distributional grounds as a way of financing local government.

■ Rates are also regressive, but they do perform a useful role in relation to the whole tax system by taxing housing. Some form of property tax is a natural choice as a local tax.

■ A Local Income Tax would be progressive and would reduce the need for Housing Benefit. It would probably be less open to evasion than the Poll Tax, but would require substantial administrative changes for its introduction.

■ The structure of local government finance resulting from the current reforms will leave local government with a very narrow discretionary base (see above), with heavy gearing between local spending and local tax rates.

Putting all of these together, Stephen Smith and Duncan Squire concluded that the search for an *alternative* to rates has been mis-directed.[15] If business rates are to be set at a uniform level — a move which has some logic behind it —

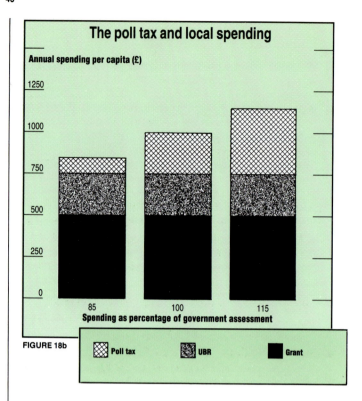

The poll tax and local spending

Annual spending per capita (£)

FIGURE 18b

Spending as percentage of government assessment

⬚ Poll tax   ⬚ UBR   ■ Grant

the need is for a *supplement* to domestic rates. Specifically, the following package would have much to commend it:

(a) Retention (or restoration) of domestic rates based on a new valuation of property (on the basis of capital rather than rental values).[16] To ease re-introduction of a property tax and to lessen the need for rebates, the yield should be rather less than that of domestic rates now.

(b) Introduction of a Local Income Tax both as a substitute for the reduced yield of rates and as a supplement to them, so as to increase the proportion of their revenues which local authorities control (to reduce the 'gearing' problem described above). To prevent damaging effects on overall marginal tax rates or the creation of a 'flight to the suburbs', there should probably be an upper limit to LIT rates.

(c) The additional revenue from the LIT would allow the aggregate size of the grant from central government to be lower and an equivalent fall in national income tax rates.

Such a package would be progressive, would restore some discretion to local government and would retain some of the better features of rates. It would be an improvement on current arrangements and a huge improvement on the Poll Tax.

19. Taxing companies

The taxation of companies raises complex issues going well beyond the scope of this book. The intention of this section is therefore simply to outline the current system and some of its main features rather than to explore it in detail.

There are four main kinds of tax levied on companies in the UK:

■ **Corporation Tax** levied on the profits of 'incorporated' companies (that is, those where the liability of the owners or shareholders is limited to their investment).

■ **Employer National Insurance Contributions** charged on the wages and salaries paid by all employers (with special arrangements for the self-employed).

■ **Non-domestic rates** paid to local authorities and charged on commercial and industrial property.

■ **North Sea taxes** charged on companies involved in oil and gas extraction (these are not discussed any further — see the section on 'Where to find out more' for references).

The problem of incidence

At first sight, it might seem obvious that companies should be taxed. Companies control much of the economy, own most of the country's assets and make large profits. They can therefore surely bear 'their share' of the tax burden. But a company in itself does not bear anything — imposing tax on it must actually affect some of the people involved in its activities.

The most obvious effect is that profits — and hence the dividends paid to the company's owners, its *shareholders* — would be reduced. But the company might respond to taxation by raising its prices, leaving profits unaffected, and **shifting** the incidence of the tax to *consumers* of its products. Equally, the effect of the tax might be that less would be available for wages — the *employees* would bear the tax; or it might pay less to its *suppliers*; or its *managers* might be provided with fewer perks and less plush offices.

All taxes are open to the problem of shifting and to difficulties in telling who really ends up paying them. But company taxes are especially vulnerable given the wide variety of directions in which they might spread and the greatly different consequences of each. If shareholders bear the tax, it will be highly progressive; if consumers bear it, its effects will be like those of an indirect tax and will be much less progressive. As the economy becomes more internationalised, the latter may become more likely; foreign investors will demand the same after-tax rate of return as they can obtain in other countries. Prices and the level of investment will tend to adjust until this is achieved. On the other hand, it may become more difficult for domestic producers to change the price at which internationally traded goods are sold, in which case, consumers will be protected.

Why tax companies at all?

In view of this uncertainty, it might seem better to avoid company taxes and instead to apply tax directly on the intended target — taxes on dividends if shareholders are the target; taxes on high salaries and fringe benefits if managers are the target; or indirect taxes if consumers are. Nonetheless, there are good reasons for retaining a system of company tax:

■ If companies were not taxed, they would provide a tax-free 'shelter' for the wealthy. Instead of saving in a taxable form, they would accumulate their savings within a company and pay no tax until the money was needed. This would not matter so much if Capital Gains Tax could be made effective — the accumulation of profits within the company would make shares in it more valuable, and tax could be charged on these capital gains. But as discussed in Sections 12 and 13, it is hard to make capital gains taxes really effective. One role of a company tax is therefore as a way of catching *undistributed* (or 'retained') profits.

■ Companies offer a convenient 'tax handle' for tax collectors to grab hold of — there are relatively few of them to deal with compared with individual taxpayers or even retailers.

■ Other countries have company taxes and their effects are built into the whole structure of international finance and into the 'double taxation' agreements between countries. The rules of some of these agreements can have the effect that the foreign *company* ends up paying the same tax (at a rate set in its home country) regardless of the level of British tax (for payments of which, the home government gives a 'credit'). If Britain charged such companies less tax, the beneficiaries would be foreign governments, not the foreign companies, so there would not necessarily even be a greater incentive for them to invest here.

■ Domestic financial markets have also adjusted to the existence of company taxes — abolishing them (or even reducing their rates) might simply deliver windfall gains to those who had already allowed for the tax.

These are considerations of principle. The major reason for the continued existence of company taxes is grubbier. Company taxes are much less visible than direct taxes on individuals or even than indirect taxes like VAT. Precisely because it is unclear who really ends up paying them, they offer a convenient way for governments to raise revenue with little protest. The wheels of the recent tax reforms in countries like the USA and Canada have been oiled by presentation of the changes as lowering the burden on individuals financed by more tax on companies. As with many aspects of the taxation system, appearances can be much more important than the underlying reality.

Corporation Tax

For profits made in the financial years since 1986–87, Corporation Tax has been charged at 35%. Until 1982–83 the rate had been 52%, but the 1984 Budget set in train a series of reductions to take it to its current level — which is, as was shown in Section 4, one of the lowest of the major western economies.

The tax is charged on taxable profits, calculated by subtracting various allowable costs from a company's income. Many of these costs and receipts are straightforward items like wages or proceeds from sales, but there are several items whose treatment is more complicated:

■ *Capital gains*, when assets are sold for more than was paid for them (after allowing for inflation), used to be taxed at a special rate of 30%. They are now taxed at the same 35% rate as other profits.

■ The increase in the value of *stocks* of materials and unsold products held by a company represents part of the company's profits. This increase is also included in taxable profits. But when prices are rising, part represents no more than the effects of inflation. A special allowance — **stock relief** — intended to remove this problem was abolished as part of the 1984 reforms.

■ Part of a business's costs take the form of the *depreciation* of the capital equipment which it owns and uses. The allowance currently given for depreciation of plant and machinery each year is 25% of whatever was left after depreciation at the end of the previous year. Before 1984, companies were able to claim an allowance for the *whole* cost of any investment when they made it, rather than spreading it out over several years as now. Note that the allowances are based on the original cash amount paid for capital equipment, not on its current value.

■ Another part of costs is the money paid to suppliers of finance. Where this takes the form of borrowing, the *interest* payable is fully deductible. Where finance comes from shareholders — 'equity capital' — the *dividends* paid out are taxed through the **imputation system** (see box).

Effects of the 1984 reforms

The 1984 reforms are an interesting example of how tax reform can be popular. The eye-catching reduction in the *rate* of Corporation Tax from 52% to 35% pleased business. However, the reforms did not necessarily reduce tax revenues because of the 'base broadening' measures like the abolition of stock relief and of the 100% investment allowances.[1]

In the short term, tax revenues certainly *rose.* It took a while for the new depreciation allowances to build up. As this was happening, companies were able to claim less in the way of allowances than they had done under the old system and so paid more tax than they would have done, even though the tax rate was being reduced.

What will happen in the long run depends crucially on the rate of inflation. If inflation is low, the abolition of stock relief and the 100% allowances will not matter much and the lower tax rate will indeed mean that revenues will be less than they would have been. But if inflation is rapid, companies will pay tax on profits resulting simply from the effects of inflation on the value of their stocks. In addition, the depreciation allowances — based on the original cash value of the investment — will not be worth so much. Higher inflation will therefore mean greater taxes, even if companies are not really making any greater profits.

Calculating the 'break-even' rate of inflation for the tax under the new system to equal what it would have been under the old one is a controversial exercise. One estimate puts it at around 8%.[2] if inflation is higher than this, the Treasury wins in the long run; if it is lower, companies win. The way in which inflation affects the tax which has to be paid has been one of the major criticisms of the new system.

Another objective of the 1984 reforms was to reduce the discrimination in the tax charged on different kinds of investment. Before the change, there were huge differences between, say, the tax charged on an investment in machinery financed by borrowing from a pension fund and that charged on commercial buildings financed by raising equity finance from higher rate taxpayers. In the first case the tax system actually *added* to the investment's return — the 'effective' tax rate was negative — while in the second it was high and positive. These kinds of differences are now much smaller than they used to be; the tax system is less important in determining what kinds of investment are made and how they are financed.[3]

At the same time, the effect of the new system has been to

The imputation system

As explained in the main text, one of the reasons for having Corporation Tax is as a way of taxing retained (undistributed) profits, given that Capital Gains Tax is ineffective. Distributed profits — dividends — are, however, caught by the income tax system as well as Corporation Tax. To mitigate this 'double taxation' of dividends, there is a special 'imputation' system.

Under this, when dividends are paid out (from profits on which Corporation Tax has already been paid) they are deemed *already to have had basic rate Income Tax paid on them.* More tax only has to be paid if the recipient is a higher rate taxpayer. Non-taxpayers like pension funds can *reclaim* the 'tax credit' at the basic rate from the Inland Revenue.

Suppose that a company has profits of £100,000 and pays out what is left after Corporation Tax (of £35,000) as dividends. Different kinds of shareholder would be affected as follows:

■ If they are *basic rate* income taxpayers, they receive the £65,000 dividend and have no further tax to pay — it counts as having been a gross dividend of £86,667 on which Income Tax of £21,667 has already been paid.

■ If *non-taxpayers*, like pension funds, they receive the £65,000 and reclaim the £21,667 'tax credit' — receiving £86,667 in all.

■ If *higher rate* taxpayers, what is deemed to be the gross dividend, £86,667, is taxed at 40%. This comes to £34,667, so they have to pay an extra £13,000 on top of the £21,667 tax credit. They therefore receive £52,000 net.

An important side effect of the system is that a change in the basic rate does not affect the net dividends received by basic rate taxpayers! A cut in the basic rate actually *reduces* the amount that pension funds receive but increases the net amount received by higher rate taxpayers.

increase the tax which would be charged on the return from a 'typical' new investment. The capital allowances given in the pre-1984 system were intended to encourage a higher level of investment; their removal will have the effect in the long run of discouraging investment, another feature which has been criticised.[4]

Problems of this kind have led to calls for the substitution of a 'Cash Flow' Corporation Tax for current arrangements. Details of these proposals can be found in the references under 'Where to find out more'.

Employer National Insurance Contributions

As well as the NICs paid by employ*ees* described in Section 7, employ*ers* also have to pay them. They are calculated in a similar way, but with a different rate schedule. As with employee contributions, a structure of reduced rates was introduced in the 1985 Budget. For 1988–89 the rates are:

Below £41 per week	Zero
£41–£69 per week	5%
£70–£104 per week	7%
£105–£154 per week	9%
Above £155 per week	10.45%

As with employee NICs, these rates are applied to the whole of earnings, so the employer NIC on a wage of £100 per week is £7. Up to £155 per week the two kinds of contribution are equal, but above this the rate for employers rises to 10.45%, compared with 9% for employees. A second difference is that there is now no upper limit for employer contributions. The same upper limit used to apply to them as to employee contributions, but it was removed in the 1985 Budget.

The effect of employer contributions is that wage costs are higher than they would be without them. To pay someone a gross weekly wage of £200 costs the employer £220.90. In theoretical terms there is little difference between a tax of this kind and a tax charged directly on the employee — both insert a 'wedge' of tax between the cost to the employer and what the employee actually receives after tax. Once again, however, appearances may be important. When the Upper Earnings Limit was removed for employers, the cost of employing highly paid people rose. If the incidence was really on employees, one might have expected top salaries to fall. This does not appear to have happened. The effect of the *change*, at least, has apparently been absorbed by employers.

National Insurance Contributions for the self-employed

The self-employed pay NICs at different rates to those applied to other employees and their employers. The amount payable depends on the income or profits they derive from their trade or business. Provided that these exceed a certain amount (£2,205 a year in 1988–89, just above the lower earnings limit for other contributions), they pay 'Class 2' contributions at a flat rate (£4.05 per week in 1988–89). On top of this, they pay 'Class 4' contributions as a percentage (6.3% since 1983–84) of income or profits *to the extent that they exceed* a lower limit (£4,750 a year in 1988–89) up to an upper limit (£15,860 a year, equivalent to the Upper Earnings Limit for normal employee contributions). Under a valuable concession introduced in the 1985 Budget, *half* of these Class 4 contributions can be claimed as an Income Tax deduction. This makes the effective Class 4 rate on a basic rate taxpayer 4.7%, and 3.8% on a higher rate taxpayer (on profits up to the upper limit).

As there is no equivalent of the employ*er* contribution, this makes the total contribution collected from a self-employed person much less than that from someone in employment with an equivalent income. This differential has increased since 1978–79, when the Class 4 contribution rate was only 1.5% below the standard employee rate, compared with 2.7% now, particularly as a result of the deductibility of half of Class 4 contributions against Income Tax. However, the National Insurance benefits to which the self-employed are entitled are very restricted — for instance, they can claim only the basic element of the state pension, not the earnings related component, and not Unemployment Benefit.

Non-domestic rates

Finally, as mentioned in the previous section, local authorities charge rates on 'non-domestic' properties. Under the Poll Tax reforms non-domestic rates will be retained. However, instead of being charged a rate set locally, the same *Uniform Business Rate* will be charged nationally. A new valuation of business properties is also being carried out to replace the current rateable values based on 1973 rents.

Businesses will therefore be affected in two ways. Those in areas where the rate poundage is currently higher than the national average will gain from the Uniform Business Rate, while those in low rate areas will lose. This has the effect of benefiting businesses in what are largely Conservative areas at the expense of those in what are largely Labour areas. But there will also be a relative shift so that businesses in areas which have become more prosperous since 1973 — where values have increased faster than the average — will pay more, while those in declining areas will pay less. In many cases this will reinforce the effects of the Uniform Business Rate.

The change to a Uniform Business Rate with the proceeds distributed between authorities in proportion to their populations also means that there has been an important change in the relative advantage to authorities of new businesses operating in their areas. Under the old system, the creation of a new non-domestic rateable value would have increased their tax base, while under the new system, their tax position will not be affected at all.

20. A strategy for reform

The rest of this book has examined the building blocks of the tax system and has suggested how they could be improved, in particular, how they could be modified to make the system more progressive while raising more revenue to finance higher benefits. These individual changes could be put together in a huge variety of ways and it is hoped that readers will now be in a position to work out roughly what the effects of their own preferred package of reforms would be.

However, changes to different parts of the system interact. One cannot therefore simply add together the revenue-raising or distributional effects of isolated changes to give the exact effect of a combined package. Changes to the Income Tax rate structure will have different effects depending on the tax treatment of husband and wife. Family Credit and Housing Benefit depend on net income, and hence on Income Tax and National Insurance Contribution (NIC) structures. It is because of such interactions that a simulation model like TAXMOD is so useful. By examining the effects of combined changes to the whole tax and benefit system on a large representative sample of families, such interactions can be allowed for.

Aims of a reform package

This section describes one example of the kind of package which can be built up using some of the reform possibilities discussed in earlier sections. Choosing the aims for such a package is difficult. In view of the great inequality in incomes described in Section 2, some people would favour a highly redistributive reform. Others would be concerned to ensure that in any reform the maximum proportion of the population gained, so as to secure widespread political support. Still others would be concerned that any reform did not run the danger of damaging the operation of the economy. The choice between such approaches, and indeed between them and the status quo, is obviously a central political issue and it is not the intention here to choose between them.

Instead, the package discussed below has been designed to provide a *benchmark* against which those with different aims can judge their own proposals and objectives. Those who favour a *greater* degree of redistribution would have to accept higher tax rates and/or more losers compared with the current position. Those who would like fewer losers and/or lower tax rates would find it difficult to achieve such a large degree of redistribution.

The benchmark objective shown is to reverse the overall distributional effects of the changes to the direct tax and benefit systems which have been made in the last 10 years (described in Section 3). Specifically, it is designed to:

■ Result in a gain of £8.50 per week per family for the bottom half of the income distribution (reversing their loss of £8.50 since 1978–79).

■ Result in gains for the clear majority of the population, avoiding, so far as possible, any losses at all for those at the bottom of the distribution.

■ Have a cost which equals no more than the £600 million which the Government is already planning to spend on the 1990 reforms to the Income Tax treatment of husband and wife (as these will be incorporated in the package).

■ Result in a tax structure which is an improvement on *both* what exists now and what existed 10 years ago.

It is the last aim which makes the exercise interesting. Simply restoring the 1978–79 tax and benefit system (uprated for changes in national income) would involve undesirable features like a top Income Tax rate of 98%. It would also involve losses for 40% of families which, while less than the 57% who would gain, could prove a significant barrier to political acceptability. What the example suggests is that both of those problems could, in fact be avoided.

The combined reform to taxes and benefits

The details of the combined reform package are given in the boxes. On the benefit side, the emphasis is on improving National Insurance benefits (the levels of benefits are intended to be representative of what could be achieved, rather than a detailed blueprint[1]). The levels of means-tested benefits are adjusted so that the numbers claiming them are reduced, while allowing those who remain dependent on them to share in gains from the package. The tax reforms include a graduated structure for Income Tax (see Section 5); the conversion of Income Tax Allowances into a Zero Rate Band (Section 6); fully independent taxation without a special allowance for married men, offset by a doubling of Child Benefit and an increase in the married pension; a progressive structure of employee NICs incorporating the major change of converting the Lower Earnings Limit into an *allowance* of £50 per week (Section 7); the re-introduction of an Investment Income Surcharge and the restriction or removal of various tax concessions and allowances (Sections 6 and 14).

Effects of the combined package

The main effects of this package are illustrated in Figures 20a, 20b and 20c (derived from TAXMOD). Overall the bottom 80% of families gain, with the average gain for those in the bottom half of the distribution at just over £8.50 per week as required. Comparing Figures 20a and 3b, it can be seen that the distributional effects of changes in direct taxes and benefits over the last 10 years are indeed reversed.

The cost of the reform is borne by those who have gained most in the last 10 years, with the top 10% losing an average of nearly £46.50 per week, a total of £7.2 billion per year (of which nearly £6 billion would come from the top 5%). Again, this reverses the gains described in Section 3.

In terms of the numbers gaining and losing, Figures 20b and 20c show that the result is much more favourable than a simple return to the 1978-79 system. Overall, more than 73% of families gain, while fewer than 23% lose. The losers are, by and large, those with the highest incomes. Within the bottom half, only 3% lose and 90% gain.[2] Ninety-seven per cent of pensioner families (married couples and single people) gain and only 3% lose.

All this is achieved within a tax structure which incorporates a top Income Tax rate of 50% and a top total marginal rate of tax of 61.5% on earnings or 65% on investment income, well within the mainstream of other OECD countries shown in Section 4. The new combined marginal rate structure for Income Tax and NICs is shown in Figure 20d (and can be compared with the current structure shown in Figure 7a). The 'spikes' from the current jumps in NIC liability are eliminated, as is the 'dip' in combined rates above the current Upper Earnings Limit. For the majority of earners with earnings below £11,000 per year, close to 'average' earnings, marginal rates are (just) lower than now.

Figure 20e shows the corresponding effects on *average* tax rates for single people compared with the current system. The rise in average tax rates is much smoother than now, and is of course, more gradual at the bottom. The 'break-even' point is, at £13,400, above 'average' earnings.

As will be remembered from Figure 2c, the great majority of the working population earns less than this, and only a minority is affected by the higher marginal rates (and fewer by the higher average rates). Taking account of benefit withdrawal as well, while 55% of men in work face a higher marginal tax rate and 43% a lower one, the rate is reduced

Benefit changes incorporated in the package

Improved pensions

Single retirement pension:	£50 per week	(£41.15 now)
Addition for spouse:	£37.25	(£24.75)
Widow's pension:	£50	(£41.15)
Age addition (over 80s):	£5	(£0.25)

These are somewhat more generous than simply restoring the pension to its 1978–79 level to take account of the abolition of Income Tax age allowances proposed below. The spouse's addition is £7.25 higher than the £30 which would be suggested by the 1.6 ratio of married couples' to single people's benefits elsewhere in the system in order to offset the effects on pensioners of the abolition of the Married Man's Tax Allowance. The age addition for the over 80's is a way of focusing extra help on those with the least entitlement to other pensions.

Improved national insurance benefits

Single invalidity pension:	£50	(£41.15)
Addition for spouse:	£30	(£24.75)
Single unemployment and sickness benefit:	£40	(£32.75/£31.30)
Additions for spouse:	£25	(£20.20/£19.40)

The invalidity pension is in line with the retirement pension (but without the extra spouse addition of £7.25 for abolition of the Married Man's Allowance). Unemployment and Sickness Benefits are restored to their 1978–79 values in relation to other incomes. In addition the disqualification penalties for Unemployment Benefit are restored to those that applied in 1978–79 (that is, 6 weeks' disqualification, rather than 26).[3]

Child Benefit and Family Credit

Child Benefit is doubled from £7.25 to £14.50, reflecting the abolition of the Married Man's Allowance. As described in

Section 9, Family Credit is adjusted so that half of the effect of this 'floats' families off the benefit (for instance, reducing the maximum for children under 10 to £2.50). One Parent Benefit is also doubled to £10 (from £4.90) to focus more help on this group.

Income Support (IS)

Single IS allowance (18 and over)	£36.50	(£33.40 over 25; £26.05 under 25)
Married couple's IS allowance	£58.30	(£51.45)
Single over 60's premium	£12	(£10.65)
Married couple's over 60's premium	£19.20	(£16.25)
(Over 80's premiums £5 higher)		
Single parent premium	£6.20	(£3.70)
Child IS allowances		
0–10	£14.50	(£10.75)
11–15	£19.75	(£16.10)
16–17	£23.05	(£19.40)

These are designed so that total allowances reflect approximately half of the improvements to non-means-tested benefits described above. The IS addition for children aged 10 or under becomes equal to the new Child Benefit rate. The rate of IS for those aged 18–25 is brought into line with that for other adults.

Housing Benefit

Maximum rate element	100%	(80%)
Rent taper	55%	(65%)
Rates taper	15%	(20%)

These remove the worst of the recent Housing Benefit cuts without unduly extending the range over which means-testing applies (it also appears that the taper for Poll Tax rebates will be set at 15% rather than the 20% which has applied to rate rebates).

Tax changes included in the package

National Insurance Contributions

Changed to a progressive structure so that contributions are calculated on the *excess* of earnings over £50 per week (equivalent to the £2,605 a year single Income Tax allowance) with no upper limit (see Section 7). The rate is set at 11.5%, so as to raise additional revenue to finance improvements in national insurance benefits (this still leaves reduced contributions for the majority of earners on less than £12,000 a year). The deductibility of half of Class 4 National Insurance Contributions against Income Tax is removed.

Income Tax

All existing personal allowances (including age allowance and Married Man's Allowance) are abolished and replaced by a Zero Rate Band of £2,605 a year for each person (see Section 6). Graduated rate structure introduced with following rates:

Income	Marginal rate
0– 2,605	Zero
2,605–11,000	22%
11,000–19,000	34%
19,000–22,000	40%
22,000–27,000	45%
over 27,000	50%

The basic rate band is broken in two and the 45% and 50% bands are restored from roughly what their starting points would have been if they had not been abolished in the 1988 Budget (as explained in Section 6, the Zero Rate Band means that they take earlier effect than they would under the allowance system). Allowing for the Zero Rate Band, this structure is equivalent to that described in Section 5.

Fully independent taxation is introduced as it will be in 1990 (see Section 10); mortgage interest tax relief is restricted to the initial rate of 22% (currently 25% for most taxpayers) and the composite rate is also set at 22% (see Section 12). Finally, an investment income surcharge (see Section 14) is reintroduced at a rate of 15% on investment income exceeding £3,000 per year (again on an individual basis).

The package also includes a total of £700 million raised by restriction or removal of various concessions such as the Business Expansion Scheme, share options and the phasing out of Life Assurance Premium Relief and tax-free lump sums for pensions (see Section 14, bearing in mind that the 'cost' of these concessions will be higher with a top rate Income Tax rate of 50%). This could either be done by directly restricting them, or by introducing a minimum tax or maximum allowance system (see Section 6).

for 53% of women and only increased for 25%. On average, the marginal rate facing men rises from 33% to over 38%, but that for women falls from over 28% to 24%. Given the greater responsiveness of the female labour supply to taxation, the net effect of this on overall labour supply could well be positive.

Given that the greatest sensitivity is at the highest rates, what may be more significant is the fall in the number facing a total marginal rate exceeding 70%: from 2.1% to 1.6% of men and from 3.0% to 1.0% of women. This is associated with a fall of 30% in the number claiming Family Credit.

The package is also successful in drastically reducing the number of pensioners on Income Support from 1.1 million to 0.2 million. In the main they are floated off Income Support but left claiming standard Housing Benefit, which is still means-tested, but appears to carry less stigma. The rever-

sal of some of the Housing Benefit cuts means that the number of non-pensioners claiming Housing Benefit rises from 0.9 to 1.1 million.

The revenue effects are shown in the table. The amounts shown are derived directly from TAXMOD, with the exception that the Income Tax increase includes £0.7 billion raised by a combination of measures to restrict the cost of various reliefs and allowances listed in the box.[4] The increase shown for Capital Gains Tax receipts occurs because the rate of tax is now tied to people's Income Tax rates (Section 12), which would now have a maximum of 50%.[5] More CGT revenue would be available if the current generous tax-free allowance of £5,000 of annual real gains was cut.

The overall net cost comes, as required, to the £0.6 billion which the Government is going to spend on introducing independent taxation of husband and wife for Income Tax in 1990 (Section 8).

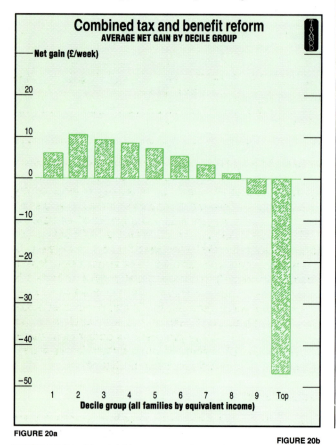

FIGURE 20a

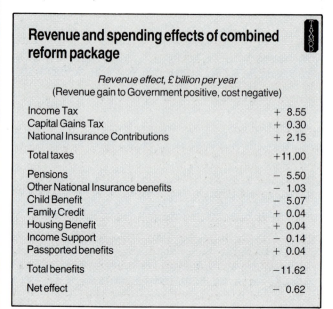

Revenue and spending effects of combined reform package

Revenue effect, £ billion per year
(Revenue gain to Government positive, cost negative)

Income Tax	+ 8.55
Capital Gains Tax	+ 0.30
National Insurance Contributions	+ 2.15
Total taxes	**+11.00**
Pensions	− 5.50
Other National Insurance benefits	− 1.03
Child Benefit	− 5.07
Family Credit	+ 0.04
Housing Benefit	+ 0.04
Income Support	− 0.14
Passported benefits	+ 0.04
Total benefits	**−11.62**
Net effect	**− 0.62**

Phasing in the reform

All of this assumes that the reform was introduced overnight in the middle of the current tax year. This is the best way of showing the effects of the 'structural' changes proposed. In reality, of course, such a change would be most likely to be

FIGURE 20b

FIGURE 20c

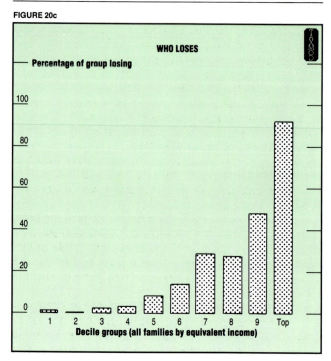

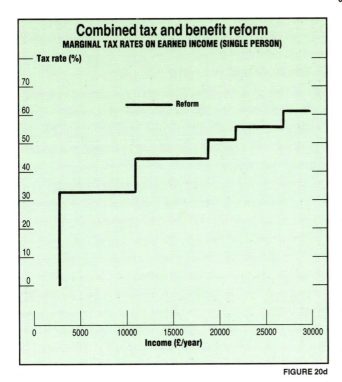

FIGURE 20d

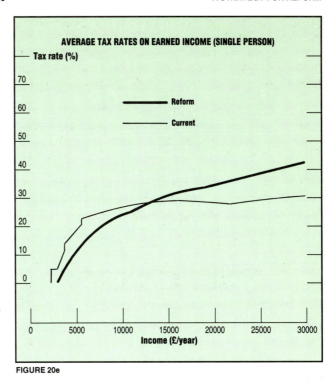

FIGURE 20e

introduced in parts and at the same time as the normal process of uprating benefits and tax allowances at the beginning of the tax year. The cash in people's hands at the moment the reform was introduced would therefore be affected by such upratings as well.

It was also suggested in Section 9 that it would be desirable to *phase out* the Married Man's Allowance (Married Couples' Allowance after 1990), rather than abolishing it overnight. One way to do this would be to freeze the cash total of the single allowance and the Married Couples' Allowance. Thus, if allowances were to be raised by 5% in general, the single allowance (or Zero Rate Band) would rise from £2,605 to £2,735. A simultaneous cut in the Married Couples' Allowance from £1,490 to £1,360 would leave the total tax-free amount for married couples constant at £4,095, protecting even childless couples from overnight losses.

The price of this would be that less would be available immediately to finance the increase in Child Benefit and the additional increase in the spouse's addition to the retirement pension. These would also have to be phased in; in this case, they could be increased by £1 over and above normal indexation in the first year of the reform. The process would be repeated at subsequent upratings until the Married Couples' Allowance had disappeared altogether and the extra addition had reached £7.25 in real terms.

A plausible scenario would be that the rest of the reform would be introduced at the beginning of a tax year, so that there would be an additional increase, say of 5% (or whatever), in the value of all benefit rates, tax bands and tax allowances as shown above (and in those not affected by the reform). The abolition of the Married Couples' Allowance and increases in Child Benefit and the married pension would be phased as just described.

If this happened, the overall proportion of families gaining would be 83%, with only 13% losing.[6] At the moment of the change, 91% of those in the bottom eight decile groups would gain and only 4% lose. More importantly, less than 1% of the bottom half of the income distribution would lose, while 92% would gain.

At the time of the change, single people earning up to £14,350 would gain. The break-even point for one-earner couples *without* children would be £15,140, and for a one-earner couple with two children, the break-even point would

be £16,140, taking account of the increase in Child Benefit.

It may be surprising, therefore, that there are any low income losers at all. The small remaining number of low income losers fall into two groups. First, there is a very small number of non-taxpayers with mortgages who lose from the cut in the rate of mortgage relief. Within the TAXMOD sample (drawn from the Family Expenditure Survey), these are self-employed people who declared very low incomes or losses ('negative incomes'). The larger group consists of two kinds of family losing out particularly from the 1990 reforms — 'breadwinner wives' (see Section 8) and some men below retirement age married to women above it. The Government has promised 'transitional' protection for both of these cases as part of the 1990 reforms to prevent them from suffering losses. The same could be done under this reform.

Conclusion

These results suggest that there *are* options for the reform of the tax system which could both finance substantial increases in benefits and leave the tax system itself more progressive and more logical in structure. Furthermore, the transition to such a system could be one from which the overwhelming majority of the population would gain. This would still leave other areas left to tackle:

■ Local taxation (see Section 18), in particular, replacement of the Poll Tax with some combination of a restored local property tax and a local income tax;

■ Taxation of wealth and inheritance (see Section 15), in particular, the replacement of the inherently ineffective Inheritance Tax with a system of recipient-based taxation;

■ Sorting out the current muddle in the taxation of savings (see Sections 12-14);

■ Creating a structure of *indirect* taxation (see Sections 16 and 17) which is unambiguously progressive, in particular, protecting the principle of zero-rating for VAT and finding a way of discouraging smoking which does not involve such a massive bite into the incomes of low income smokers.

'Tax reform' need not be a phrase used to describe tax cuts for those on the highest incomes. It could mean the construction of a fairer system for the whole population.

Where to find out more

This book is intended to serve as an introduction to the way in which the tax system works and some of the ways in which it could be reformed. It does not go into detail on all of the topics covered and some issues are omitted altogether. In addition, taxation is a highly contentious subject so that it would not be hard to find dissenters from the opinions expressed here. This section is therefore intended to suggest where the reader could go to find out more about the subjects covered in each section and where to find alternative views.

By far the most readable guide to the tax system is *The British Tax System* by John Kay and Mervyn King (Oxford University Press, 4th edition, 1986 — a 5th edition is due in 1989; henceforth *Kay and King*). This goes into more detail on nearly every subject covered here and argues persuasively for a programme of reform which has some elements in common with the approach advocated here.

Two major sources of analysis of the tax system are the Institute for Fiscal Studies (IFS) at 180/182 Tottenham Court Road, London W1P 9LE, and the ESRC Programme of research into Taxation, Incentives and the Distribution of Income (TIDI) at the Suntory-Toyota International Centre for Economics and Related Disciplines at the London School of Economics (ST/ICERD, LSE, 10 Portugal Street, London WC2A 2HD). IFS produces a regular journal, *Fiscal Studies*, and a *Report Series* and *Commentaries* covering particular topics. The TIDI programme produces a *Discussion Paper* series and ST/ICERD produces a series of *Occasional Papers*. One of these, *Tax-Benefit Models* edited by A.B. Atkinson and Holly Sutherland (ST/ICERD Occasional Paper No.10, 1988), contains a number of articles describing the construction and use of simulation models of the tax and benefit systems, including TAXMOD whose results are used throughout this book.

1. How the tax system fits together

The most useful Government source on the tax changes planned for each year is the annual *Financial Statement and Budget Report*, the 'Red Book' published by HMSO for the Treasury at the time of the Budget (usually in March). This contains forecasts of tax revenues, an account of the changes announced in the Budget and information about their revenue consequences. The Government also publishes a whole sheaf of press releases at the time of the Budget providing greater detail on the changes and its arguments for them. Information about the National Insurance Contribution system and a 'ready reckoner' for the revenue effects of possible changes in the forthcoming Budget are contained in the annual *Autumn Statement* published by the Treasury in November each year.

Official statistics on tax collections can be found in the annual *Inland Revenue Statistics* (HMSO) for Income Tax and capital taxes and in the annual *Report of the Commissioners of HM Customs and Excise* (HMSO, the most recent was Command Paper Cm 238) for indirect taxes. Figures on tax collection can also be found in the monthly *Financial Statistics* (HMSO).

The rules of the tax system as it affects the ordinary taxpayer are described in a whole series of annual publications and tax guides. The *Which? Tax Saving Guide* is always both clear and informative, particularly for those who want to make best use of many of the concessions which this book recommends an end to. The guides, published by Tolleys, to Income Tax, Corpora-tion Tax and National Insurance Contributions give comprehensive detail on direct taxes.

2. The poor and the rich

The Economics of Inequality by A.B. Atkinson (Oxford University Press, 2nd edition, 1983) gives the most useful introduction to the whole subject of income and wealth distribution. Readings on income distribution are contained in *The Personal Distribution of Incomes* (George Allen and Unwin, 1976) and *Wealth, Income and Inequality* (Oxford University Press, 2nd edition, 1980) both edited by the same author. The latter contains the celebrated 'parade of dwarfs and a few giants' by J. Pen from his book *Income Distribution* (Penguin, 1971), which illustrates the grotesque scale of inequality in income distribution by reference to a parade of people whose heights have been stretched or squashed in proportion to their incomes. *The Rich Get Richer* by John Rentoul (Unwin Paperbacks, 1987) contains a non-technical account of much of this evidence.

The Royal Commission on the Distribution of Income and Wealth produced a number of reports until its abolition in 1979, of which *Report No.7* (Cmnd.7595, HMSO, July 1979) contains some of the most useful information. More recent statistics are given in the irregular Inland Revenue *Survey of Personal Incomes* (HMSO) and 3-yearly articles in *Economic Trends* (HMSO) on the 'Distribution of Income in the United Kingdom' (the most recent was in the November 1987 issue). *Economic Trends* also contains an annual article on the 'Effects of Taxes and Benefits on Household Income' (the most recent year covered was 1985 in the November 1986 and July 1987 issues). These latter figures are further examined in *Family Fortunes: Parent's Incomes in the 1980's* by Jo Roll (Family Policy Studies Centre, 1988).

On the more specific subject of poverty, the Child Poverty Action Group's journal *Poverty* contains a regular round-up of recent statistics which have emerged from Parliamentary Question answers as well as articles discussing the latest developments. Much of this evidence is summarised in its briefing paper, *Poverty: the Facts* (CPAG, October 1988). The Group also publishes the *Poverty Publication* series (of which this book is part) on particular issues. One of these, *The Growing Divide* edited by Alan Walker and Carol Walker (CPAG, June 1987) contains articles covering many aspects of the growth in inequality between 1979 and 1987. *Poor Britain* by Joanna Mack and Stewart Lansley (George Allen and Unwin, 1985) contains the results of a 1983 survey into what poverty actually means in terms of the things people go without. Peter Townsend's monumental *Poverty in the United Kingdom* (Penguin, 1979) contains the results of a detailed survey carried out in 1968–69 and much else besides. Changes in poverty between 1899 and 1983 are analysed by David Piachaud in an article in the July 1988 *Journal of Social Policy*.

3. What has happened to the tax system since 1979?

An official view of the changes since 1979 can be found in Ian Byatt's contribution on the 'United Kingdom' in *World Tax Reform: A Progress Report* edited by Joseph A. Pechman (Brookings Institution, Washington DC, 1988). The Institute for Fiscal Studies publishes a 'Green Budget' at the beginning of each year as one of its *Commentaries*, setting out the issues which are likely to be central to the Budget, and articles in the issue of *Fiscal Studies* immediately following it describe the effects of the changes announced each year (the most recent is the May 1988 issue). The Financial Markets Group (FMG) at the London School of Economics has more recently started to publish commentaries on the Budget; see, for instance, *The 1988 Budget and Prospects for 1989* by Mervyn King and Mark Robson (FMG Discussion Paper No.31, 1988).

4. An international comparison

World Tax Reform: A Progress Report edited by Joseph A. Pechman (Brookings Institution, Washington DC, 1988) contains accounts of the recent wave of tax reform in eleven countries up to the end of 1987. For an account of the US tax system see the same author's *Federal Tax Policy* (Brookings Institution, 5th edition 1987) and for its recent reform, see his article 'Tax Reform: Theory and Practice' in *Economic Perspectives*, Summer 1987. Descriptions of the tax systems in eight major economies are given in *Comparative Tax Systems: Europe, Canada and Japan* also edited by Joseph Pechman (Tax Analysts, Arlington, 1987). A comparison of the French and British income tax systems is given in Chapter 14 of *Tax-Benefit Models* edited by A.B. Atkinson and Holly Sutherland (ST/ICERD Occasional Paper No.10, London School of Economics, 1988). The Government's Green Paper, *The Reform of Personal Taxation*, (Cmnd 9756, HMSO, 1986) contains information on family taxation systems in a number of OECD countries.

Statistics on tax collections in other countries are published in *Revenue Statistics of OECD Member Countries* (OECD, Paris) and the Central Statistical Office publishes a regular article comparing tax structures in *Economic Trends* (the most recent being in the December 1987 issue). For statistics on a wider selection of countries, see *Government Finance Statistics* published annually by the International Monetary Fund (Washington DC). Details of the personal taxation systems in most of the world are given in *Individual Taxes: A Worldwide Summary* published annually by the accountants Price Waterhouse.

4–6. Income Tax and National Insurance Contributions

The issues covered here also discussed in Chapters 1, 2 and 3 of *Kay and King*. The research evidence on the relationship between tax cuts and labour supply is summarised by Jonathan Leape in the July 1988 *Economic Report* published by the Employment Institute (Southbank House, Black Prince Road, London SE1 7SJ). For the effects of top rate Income Tax cuts in particular, see the November 1988 issue of *Fiscal Studies*. A highly technical account of the theoretical background to the design of taxation policy in general is contained in *Lectures in Public Economics* by A.B. Atkinson and J.E. Stiglitz (McGraw Hill, 1980).

For a proposal for integration of Income Tax and NICs see *Tax Reform: Options for the Third Term* edited by Bill Robinson (IFS Commentary, November 1987). For the Government's reasons for rejecting integration see the 1986 Green Paper, *The Reform of Personal Taxation* (Cmnd 9756, HMSO). For a discussion of this and other issues connected with Income Tax structure see the Meacher Committee report on *The Structure of Personal Income Taxation and Income Support* by the Treasury and Civil Service Select Committee of the House of Commons (House of Commons Paper 386 of 1982–83, HMSO) and the evidence submitted to the Committee by a wide range of organisations and individuals (House of Commons Paper 20–I of 1982–83). For information on the cost of tax allowances and 'tax expenditures' see the Government's annual Public Expenditure White Paper (the most recent information is in Table 6.5 of Cm 288–I, HMSO, January 1988). On specific issues: for the Income Tax age allowance, see the article by Nick Morris in the November 1981 issue of *Fiscal Studies*; for arguments *against* the kind of graduation in the rate structure suggested here, see the article by Andrew Dilnot and Nick Morris in the November 1987 issue; and for issues connected with tax evasion, see *Britain's Shadow Economy* by Stephen Smith (Oxford University Press, 1986).

8 and 9. Taxation of husband and wife

The principles of choosing the tax unit are discussed in Chapter 18 of the Meade Committee Report, *The Structure and Reform of Direct Taxation* (George Allen and Unwin, 1978). They are also discussed within the whole context of family property law in *Property and Marriage: An Integrated Approach* by Judith Freedman, Elizabeth Hammond, Judith Masson and Nick Morris (IFS Report Series No.29, 1988). The article by Richard Blundell and others in the November 1984 *Fiscal Studies* examines the labour supply effects of different family taxation systems in detail.

The Government has published two Green Papers on the subject, *The Taxation of Husband and Wife* (Cmnd 8093, HMSO 1980) and *The Reform of Personal Taxation* (Cmnd 9756, HMSO 1986); the actual reform which will happen in 1990 has little connection with either. The response to the 1980 Green Paper is summarised is an article by John Kay and Catherine Sandler in *Fiscal Studies*, November 1982. Options for reform are also discussed by A.B. Atkinson and Holly Sutherland in Chapter 12 of *Tax-Benefit Models* (ST/ICERD Occasional Paper No.10, LSE, 1988) and in *Tax Reform: Options for the Third Term* edited by Bill Robinson (IFS, November 1987). The reform proposed for 1990 is discussed by Bill Robinson and Graham Stark in *Fiscal Studies*, May 1988. For a discussion of the systems in other European countries, see the article by Nicola Spencer in the August 1986 *Fiscal Studies*.

10–11. Tax and social security

This subject is also discussed in Chapter 7 of *Kay and King* and Chapter 13 of the Meade Committee Report, *The Structure and Reform of Direct Taxation* (George Allen and Unwin, 1978). *Poverty and Incentives* by Richard Hemming (Oxford University Press, 1984) describes all aspects of the social security system and possibilities for reform. An earlier discussion of the issues is in *Poverty in Britain and the Reform of Social Security* by A.B. Atkinson (Cambridge University Press, 1970). The literature on social security is comprehensively surveyed in 'Income maintenance and social insurance: a survey' by the same author in Volume II of the *Handbook of Public Economics* edited by A. Auerbach and M.S. Feldstein (North Holland, 1985).

The Reform of Social Security by Andrew Dilnot, John Kay and Nick Morris (Oxford University Press, 1984) analyses the relationship between taxation and social security in detail, advocating a very different approach to that suggested in this book. In particular, the authors argue strongly for integration of the tax and benefit systems and for a switch from universal Child Benefit and pensions towards income related benefits administered through the tax system. See also the article by Andrew Dilnot, Graham Stark and Steven Webb in the February 1987 *Fiscal Studies*. The subject is also one of the central issues discussed in the Meacher Committee report, *The Structure of Personal Income Taxation and Income Support* and in the evidence submitted to the committee (House of Commons Papers 386 and 20-I of 1982–83, HMSO). CPAG's evidence is reprinted in *The Poverty of Taxation* edited by Alan Walker (Poverty Pamphlet 56, 1982). The effects of integration proposals are covered in Chapters 12 and 13 of *Tax-Benefit Models* edited by A.B. Atkinson and Holly Sutherland (ST/ICERD Occasional Paper No.10, LSE, 1988). The specific issue of moving towards a social dividend system is discussed by the same authors in *Integrating Income Taxation and Social Security: Analysis of a Partial Basic Income* (TIDI Discussion Paper No.123, LSE, 1988). Proposals for a form of social dividend are given in *Instead of the Dole: An Inquiry into the Integration of the Tax and Benefit Systems* by Hermione Parker (Routledge, forthcoming).

The government's proposals for the reform of social security are described in its Green Paper, *Reform of Social Security* (Cmnd 9517, HMSO, London 1985) and its subsequent White Paper, *Reform of Social Security: Programme for Action* (Cmnd 9691, HMSO, 1985). Its views on integration of tax and benefits are discussed in the 1986 Green paper *The Reform of Personal Taxation* (Cmnd 9756, HMSO). The effects of the reforms actually carried out in 1988 are discussed by Andrew Dilnot and Steven Webb in the August 1988 issue of *Fiscal Studies* and by Hermione Parker in *Effects of Mr John Moore's April 1988 Benefit Changes* (Welfare State Programme Research Note

No.10, ST/ICERD, London School of Economics, 1988).

The more general effects of social security changes since 1979 are discussed in Chapters 10–13 of *The Growing Divide* edited by Alan Walker and Carol Walker (CPAG, 1987). What has happened to benefits for the unemployed is dissected in gory detail in *Turning the Screw: Benefits for the Unemployed 1979–1988* by A.B. Atkinson and John Micklewright (TIDI Discussion Paper No.121, LSE, 1988). The specific issue of the future of Child Benefit is examined in *Child Benefit: Investing in the Future* by Joan Brown (CPAG, 1988). The problems of housing benefits are described by John Hills and Richard Hemming in an article in the March 1983 *Fiscal Studies*. The problems of take-up of social security benefits are discussed in an article by Vanessa Fry and Graham Stark in the November 1987 *Fiscal Studies*.

The specific rules of the social security system are detailed in CPAG's two annual reference volumes, the *National Welfare Benefits Handbook* (18th edition for 1988-89 by Beth Lakhani, Jan Luba, Anna Ravetz, Jim Read and Penny Wood) and the *Rights Guide to Non-Means-Tested Social Security Benefits* (11th edition for 1988–89 by Mark Rowland). The details of the system are also given in *Tolley's Social Security*. Statistics on the subject are given in the annual *Social Security Statistics* (HMSO) and section 15 of the latest Public Expenditure White Paper (Cm 288-II, HMSO, 1988) contains a great deal of information on social security spending and performance, including revelations such as the finding that only 35% of letters about Supplementary Benefit sent out by DHSS local offices in 1987 were actually of a 'satisfactory' standard.

12–14. Taxation of investment income and capital gains

The problems of taxing income from capital and the arguments for replacing current arrangements with an Expenditure Tax are central concerns of *Kay and King* (see in particular, Chapters 4, 5 and 6) and of the Meade Committee Report, *The Structure and Reform of Direct Taxation*, especially Chapters 3–10 (George Allen and Unwin, 1978). Nicholas Kaldor's *An Expenditure Tax* (Allen and Unwin, 1955) started the modern debate on the subject. Contributions on both sides of the debate are contained in *What Should be Taxed: Income or Expenditure?* edited by Joseph A. Pechman (Brookings Institution, Washington DC, 1980). For more recent views of the same issues and of the reality of taxes as a hybrid, see *Uneasy Compromise* edited by H.J. Aaron, H. Galper and J.A. Pechman (Brookings Institution, 1988). For proposals for a separate flat rate tax on investment income see *Prospects for Tax Reform in 1988* by Mervyn King and *The 1988 Budget and Prospects for 1989* by Mervyn King and Mark Robson (FMG Discussion Papers No.10, 1987 and No.31, 1988, LSE). For details of the treatment of different kinds of saving in Britain see *Savings and Fiscal Privilege* by John Hills (IFS Report Series No.9, 1984). For the interaction between company taxation and the taxation of savings in Sweden, the UK, the USA and West Germany, see *The Taxation of Income from Capital* edited by M.A. King and D. Fullerton (University of Chicago Press, 1984). The Capital Gains Tax system is discussed in an article by John King in the May 1985 issue of *Fiscal Studies*. The problems surrounding pension funds are analysed in *Taxing Pensions* by Vanessa Fry, Elizabeth Hammond and John Kay (IFS Report Series No.14, 1985). For the taxation of housing, see M.A. King and A.B. Atkinson's article in the Spring 1980 *Midland Bank Review*. For the taxation of life insurance, see the consultative document, *The Taxation of Life Assurance* (Inland Revenue, 1988).

15. Taxing wealth and inheritance

For an analysis of the distribution of wealth see *Distribution of personal wealth in Britain* by A.B. Atkinson and A.J. Harrison (Cambridge University Press, 1978). Some of the estimates in this are updated in *Trends in the Distribution of Wealth in Britain 1923–1981* by A.B. Atkinson, J. Gordon and A.J. Harrison (TIDI Discussion Paper No.70, LSE, 1986). The reports of the Royal Commission on the Distribution of Income and Wealth cover the subject in detail (see, for instance, its *Report No.7*, Cmnd 7595, HMSO, 1979). The Government's regular series of estimates on wealth distribution are contained in the annual *Inland Revenue Statistics* (HMSO). A number of articles on wealth distribution are contained in *Wealth, Income and Inequality* edited by A.B. Atkinson (Oxford University Press, 2nd edition, 1980). The subject is also explored at a less technical level together with proposals for the redistribution of wealth in *Unequal Shares* by the same author (Penguin, revised edition, 1974). A more recent account of the material is in *The Rich Get Richer* by John Rentoul (Unwin Paperbacks, 1987).

The taxation of wealth and inheritance is discussed in Chapters 15 and 16 of the Meade Committee Report, *The Structure and Reform of Direct Taxation* (George Allen and Unwin, 1978) and in *An Annual Wealth Tax* by C.T. Sandford, J.R.M. Willis and D.J. Ironside (Heinemann, 1975). An account of the lingering death of Capital Transfer Tax is given by Alister Sutherland in the November 1981 and August 1984 editions of *Fiscal Studies* and proposals for a recipient based transfer tax are outlined by Cedric Sandford in the November 1987 issue.

16 and 17. Indirect taxes

These are discussed in Chapters 8 and 15 of *Kay and King*. Statistics and information on indirect taxes are given in the annual report of the Commissioners of HM Customs and Excise (that for 1986–87 is Cm 238, HMSO, 1987). Estimates of the incidence of indirect taxes are given in the annual *Economic Trends* articles on 'The Effects of Taxes and Benefits on Household Income' (see the November 1986 and July 1987 issues for the 1985 results). The theoretical debate about patterns of indirect taxation is discussed in detail in Lecture 12 of *Lectures on Public Economics* by A.B. Atkinson and J.E. Stiglitz (McGraw Hill, 1980). See also *Who Pays Indirect Taxes?* by Catherine Lee and Panos Pashardes (IFS Report Series No. 32, 1988).

The European Commission's proposals are described in *Fiscal Harmonisation: An Analysis of the European Commission's Proposals* by Catherine Lee, Mark Pearson and Stephen Smith (IFS Report Series No.28, 1988) and in *The Revenue and Welfare Effects of Fiscal Harmonisation for the UK* by Elizabeth Symons and Ian Walker (IFS Working Paper No.88/8). Proposals for the extension of the VAT base with distributional consequences offset by changes in benefits and tax allowances are given in an article by Evan Davies and John Kay in the February 1985 issue of *Fiscal Studies*.

The structure of tobacco taxation, in particular the choice between specific and *ad valorem* rates of tax, is discussed in *The Structure of Tobacco Taxes in the European Community* by John Kay and Michael Keen (IFS Report Series No.1, 1982) and in *Changing Patterns of Smoking: Are There Economic Causes?* by Vanessa Fry and Panos Pashardes (IFS Report Series No.30, 1988). The determinants of spending on alcohol are examined in *Expenditure on Alcoholic Drink by Households: Evidence from the Family Expenditure Survey 1970–1980* by A.B. Atkinson, J. Gomulka and N.H. Stern (TIDI Discussion Paper 60, LSE, 1984; updated as Discussion Paper 114, 1988).

18. Rates, the Poll Tax and Local Income Tax

Principles of local taxation are discussed in Chapter 9 of *Kay and King*. The Government's arguments for the Poll Tax are very clearly presented in its Green Paper, *Paying for Local Government* (Cmnd 9714, HMSO, 1986). Its earlier ideas, rejecting a poll tax, are in *Alternatives to Domestic Rates* (Cmnd 8449, HMSO, 1981). The impact of the Poll Tax is described in *A Tax on All The People* by Carey Oppenheim (CPAG, 1987), in *Local Taxes and Local Government* by Stephen Smith and Duncan Squire (IFS Report Series No.25, 1987) and in *Who Will be*

Paying for Local Government? by the same authors (IFS Commentary, March 1986). An examination of the practicalities of a local income tax is in *Administrative Options for a Local Income Tax* by John Kay and Stephen Smith (IFS Commentary, 1987).

The major study of local government finance and taxation was the Layfield Committee's report (Cmnd 5116, HMSO, 1976). A very clear introduction to the way local government finance works is *Local Government Finance: A Practical Guide* by Ian Douglas and Steve Lord (Local Government Information Unit, 1–5 Bath Street, London EC1V 9QQ, 1986) and an account of the way the system has evolved is in *The Politics of Local Government Finance* by Tony Travers (Allen and Unwin, 1986).

19. Taxing companies

This is covered in Chapters 10 and 11 of *Kay and King* and Chapter 12 of the Meade Committee report, *The Structure and Reform of Direct Taxation* (George Allen and Unwin, 1978). It is examined in more detail in *Public Policy and the Corporation* by Mervyn King (Chapman and Hall, 1977) and *The Taxation of Income from Capital* edited by M.A. King and D. Fullerton (University of Chicago Press, 1984). The case for a cash flow tax is discussed by Mervyn King in *The Cash Flow Corporate Income Tax* (TIDI Discussion Paper No.95, LSE, 1986).

An official view of the effects of the 1984 Corporation Tax reform is in Ian Byatt's contribution to *World Tax Reform: A Progress Report* edited by Joseph A. Pechman (Brookings Institution, Washington DC, 1988). Commentaries on the reform are contained in Jeremy Edwards' article in the May 1984 *Fiscal Studies, Corporation Tax* by Michael Devereux and Colin Mayer (IFS Report Series No.11, 1984), *Inflation: the Achilles' Heel of Corporation Tax* by John King and Charles Wookey (IFS Report Series No.26, 1987) and in articles by Michael Devereux in the May 1987 and February 1988 editions of *Fiscal Studies*.

For a discussion of the issues involved in taxing oil and gas production in the North Sea, see Chapter 12 of *Kay and King* and *North Sea Taxation for the 1990s* by Stephen Bond, Michael Devereux and Michael Saunders (IFS Report Series No.27, 1987).

20. A strategy for reform

Kay and King, the Meade Committee report and the Meacher Committee Report (HC 386 of 1982–83, HMSO) all contain plans for fundamental reform of the tax system in one way or another. CPAG's evidence to the Meacher Committee containing its own proposals is in *The Poverty of Taxation* edited by Alan Walker (Poverty Pamphlet 56, 1982). Recent alternative proposals for reform can be found in *Tax Reform: Options for the Third Term* edited by Bill Robinson (IFS Commentary, 1987), *The 1988 Budget and Prospects for 1989* by Mervyn King and Mark Robson (Financial Markets Group Discussion Paper No.31, LSE, 1988) and John Kay in the November 1986 *Fiscal Studies*.

Notes

Introduction

1. Figures refer to Gross Domestic Product (at factor cost; average estimate) taken from *Economic Trends Annual Supplement 1988* (HMSO, 1988) with forecast for 1988 taken from *Financial Statement and Budget Report 1988–89* (HM Treasury, 1988, p33).
2. The version of the model used was TAXMOD 6.4 as amended up to September 1988. The model and its use are described by A.B. Atkinson and Holly Sutherland in Chapter 3 of *Tax-Benefit Models* (ST/ICERD Occasional Paper No.10, London School of Economics, 1988).

Section 1

1. *Financial Statement and Budget Report 1988–89*, Table 1.2. National income is taken as GDP at market prices from Table 2.6.
2. *Inland Revenue Statistics 1987* (HMSO, 1987) Table 1.1.
3. *Hansard* 17 May 1988, Cols WA 423–430.
4. The relationship used by the Government is a simple linear one between disposable income and payments of each indirect tax.

Section 2

1. 'The Distribution of Income in the United Kingdom 1984/85', *Economic Trends* November 1987; equivalent article in February 1981 *Economic Trends;* and *Report No.7* of the Royal Commission on the Distribution of Income and Wealth (HMSO, Cmnd 7595, 1979), Table A1. The break in the series reflects a change in the treatment of mortgage payments.
2. 'The Effects of Taxes and Benefits on Household Income 1985', *Economic Trends* July 1987, Table P. The two series shown here — original income and income after cash benefits and all taxes — are not affected by changes in definition between the two years. The intermediate series published there — gross income and disposable income — are affected by the change to Housing Benefit in 1982–83.
3. *Households below average income: a statistical analysis 1981–85* (DHSS, May 1988), Table A1, records a *rise* in the share of the bottom 10% of individuals in the income distribution from 4.1% to 4.2% between 1981 and 1985. There are two main reasons for the apparent difference between the two official sources. First, the DHSS figures are for disposable income, after allowing for direct taxes, but not after allowing for the rise in *indirect* taxes. Secondly, they miss out the 1979 to 1981 period when the major rise in unemployment — and hence fall in the share of those on low incomes — took place.
4. Quoted in *Economics* by Paul A. Samuelson (McGraw Hill, 6th edition, 1964).
5. Figures from *New Earnings Survey 1987* (HMSO, 1987), Part B, Table 37. Figures are for all full-time employees on adult rates (including those whose pay was affected by absence).
6. Ibid, Table 30 (figure excludes those whose pay was affected by absence).
7. Results drawn from TAXMOD.
8. *Family Expenditure Survey 1986* (HMSO, 1988), Table 1. Single retired adults are 14.5% of the total and more than half of these are women.

Section 3

1. Figures derived from *Financial Statement and Budget Report 1988–89*, Table 1.2, and equivalents for earlier years supplemented by *Financial Statistics*, May 1983 (HMSO, 1983).
2. Ibid.
3. *Economic Trends Annual Supplement 1988.*
4. *Hansard* 18 May 1988.
5. As footnote 1. The increase in gross rates before allowing for rebates will have been even faster, as the figures given will have been affected by the change in the Housing Benefit system in 1982–83.
6. *The Government's Expenditure Plans 1988–89 to 1990–91* (HMSO, Cm 288–I, 1988), Table 5.9, p98. Figure is for local authority spending included in the public spending planning total.
7. 1988–89 figure from Cm 288–I, p.73. 1978–79 figure from *The Politics of Local Government Finance* by Tony Travers (Allen and Unwin, 1986), Appendix Table 9, p213.
8. As footnote 1.
9. As footnote 1.
10. As footnote 3.

Section 4

1. 'International Comparisons of Taxes and Social Security Contributions in 20 OECD countries 1975–1985', *Economic Trends*, December 1987. Recent figures for Luxembourg are not available, so it is omitted here.
2. Ibid, Table 1.
3. Ibid, Table 4.
4. See *World Tax Reform: A Progress Report* edited by Joseph A. Pechman (Brookings Institution, Washington DC, 1988).

Section 5

1. This result and those below derived from TAXMOD.
2. See R.W. Blundell and I. Walker, 'Modelling the Joint Determination of Household Labour Supplies and Commodity Demands', *Economic Journal*, Vol 92, 1982. For a summary of the evidence on labour supply, see Jonathan Leape's article in the Employment Institute's *Economic Report*, July 1988.
3. Avoidance is legal; evasion is illegal. For a detailed discussion of the scale of the latter, see *Britain's Shadow Economy* by Stephen Smith (Oxford University Press, 1986).

Section 6

1. *Hansard* 29 April 1988, Cols WA 325–326.
2. There would have to be a 'Married Man's Zero Rate Band' and special arrangements for the taxation of married women's earnings.
3. *Hansard* 18 May 1988.
4. *Survey of Personal Incomes 1984–85* (HMSO, 1987), Table 4.
5. See, for instance, 'Progressivity and Graduation in Income Tax' by A.W. Dilnot and C.N. Morris, *Fiscal Studies*, November 1984.
6. The latest is Table 6.5 in *The Government's Expenditure Plans 1988–89 to 1990–91* (Cm 288–I, HMSO, 1988).

Section 7

1. *Hansard* 21 October 1988, Col WA 1029.
2. This and other results below derived from TAXMOD.
3. Cmnd 9756 (HMSO, 1986), Chapter 7.
4. See, for instance, *Tax Reform: Options for the Third Term* edited by Bill Robinson (IFS Commentary, November 1987), Chapter 3.

Section 8

1. Section 37, Income and Corporation Act 1970.
2. Derived from TAXMOD. The Government's estimate for its cost in 1990–91 is £665 million (Inland Revenue Press Release, 'Independent Taxation of Husband and Wife', 15 March 1988).
3. Derived from TAXMOD.

Section 9

1. See 'On the Reform of the Taxation of Husband and Wife: Are Incentives Important?' by R.W. Blundell, C. Meghir, E. Symons and I. Walker, *Fiscal Studies*, November 1984.
2. See, for instance, Chapter 14 of *Tax-Benefit Models* edited by A.B. Atkinson and Holly Sutherland (ST/ICERD Paper No.10, London School of Economics).
3. *The Taxation of Husband and Wife* (Cmnd 8093, 1980) and *The Reform of Personal Taxation* (Cmnd 9756, 1986).
4. See, for instance, 'The Taxation of Husband and Wife: A View of the Debate in the Green Paper' by J.A. Kay and C. Sandler, *Fiscal Studies*, November 1982.
5. This result and those below derived from TAXMOD.
6. This will include the wife's component of the married pension, currently taxed as part of the husband's income, if it is derived from his contributions.
7. See 'The Age Allowance' by C.N. Morris, *Fiscal Studies*, November 1981.
8. Cm 288–I, Table 6.5.

9. Derived from TAXMOD. Result does not take account of changes in the *composite* rate of tax which would result from the fall in the proportion of bank and building society investors who would be taxpayers.

Section 10

1. Or in certain cases — such as young people at school for the year in which they are 16 — been 'credited' with contributions while out of the workforce.
2. Sources: Cm 288–I and II, Tables 2.7, 5.2, 15.1 and 18.1 and equivalents in Cmnd 8789. Statutory Sick Pay for 1988–89 based on estimate of 8.5% growth on 1987–88 figure of £737 million. For a more detailed discussion, see 'What happened to spending on the welfare state?' by John Hills in *The Growing Divide* edited by Alan Walker and Carol Walker (CPAG, 1987).
3. These figures and those below taken from Cm 288–II, pp272–273.
4. Certain sources of income are ignored in this calculation.
5. No account is taken of 'passported' benefits such as free prescriptions for those receiving Income Support or Family Credit.
6. *Hansard* 18 May 1988, Col WA 504.
7. *Hansard* 21 October 1987, Col WA 809 and 19 November 1987, Cols WA 647–648.

Section 11

1. This is not to argue that they are high enough to start with.
2. See, for instance, *The Structure of Income Taxation and Income Support*, Third Special Report from the Treasury and Civil Service Committee (House of Commons Paper 386 of 1982–83) and 'The Targeting of Benefits: Two Approaches' by Andrew Dilnot, Graham Stark and Steven Webb, *Fiscal Studies*, February 1987.
3. Or, indeed, other conditions, such as contribution records or requirements to 'sign on' for benefits.
4. See *The Reform of Social Security* by Andrew Dilnot, John Kay and Nick Morris (Oxford University Press, 1984).
5. Cm 288–II, pp271–272.
6. See 'The Middle Classes and the Defence of the British Welfare State' by Julian Le Grand and David Winter in *Not Only the Poor* edited by R.E. Goodin and J. Le Grand (Allen and Unwin, 1987).
7. *Social Insurance and Allied Services* (HMSO, Cmd 6404, 1942).
8. Cm 288–II, Table 15.6.
9. See Chapter 6 of *The Reform of Personal Taxation*, Cmnd 9756 (HMSO, 1986).
10. As footnote 4.
11. *Instead of the Dole: An Inquiry into the Integration of the Tax and Benefit Systems* by Hermione Parker (Routledge, forthcoming).
12. See *Unemployment Benefits and Unemployment Duration* by A.B. Atkinson and John Micklewright (ST/ICERD Occasional Paper No.6, London School of Economics, 1985).
13. 'Income maintenance and social insurance: a survey' by A.B. Atkinson in the *Handbook of Public Economics* (edited by A. Auerbach and M.S. Feldstein (North Holland, 1985).

Section 12

1. 'The Distribution of Income in the United Kingdom 1984–85', *Economic Trends*, November 1987, Tables A and D.
2. *The Survey of Personal Incomes 1984–85* (HMSO, 1987), Tables 4 and 15.
3. *United Kingdom National Accounts 1987* (HMSO, 1987), Table 11.2. Figure does not include 'non-marketable tenancy rights'.
4. *The Survey of Personal Incomes 1984–85*, Table 4 and *Inland Revenue Statistics 1987*, Table 8.1.
5. For more details see *Savings and Fiscal Privilege* by John Hills (IFS Report Series No.9, 1984).
6. As footnote 3.
7. Ibid and *Savings and Fiscal Privilege*, Table 3.1.
8. *The Taxation of Life Assurance*, Inland Revenue, 1980.
9. The linkage of Capital Gains Tax rates to Income Tax rates in the 1988 Budget is, however, a useful move to limit the attractiveness of this.
10. *Savings and Fiscal Privilege*, Table 3.5.

Section 13

1. See the Meade Committee Report, pp148–149.
2. This problem with a Comprehensive Income Tax could be avoided partially if interest is treated as a wholly different category remaining taxed and deducted in nominal terms throughout the system. The overall level of gross interest rates would then adjust for this tax treatment. This would, however, only adjust for one tax rate — if

there were multiple tax rates (including tax-free institutions), the position could not be neutral for all taxpayers.
3. See, for instance, *The British Tax System* by John Kay and Mervyn King (Oxford University Press, 4th edition, 1986) and the Meade Committee Report, *The Structure and Reform of Direct Taxation* (George Allen and Unwin, 1978).
4. See *Uneasy Compromise* edited by H.J. Aaron, H. Galper and J. Pechman (Brookings Institution, Washington DC, 1988).
5. See the references under 'Where to find out more' for Section 19.

Section 14

1. This figure and those below from Cm 288–I, Table 6.5.
2. But see footnote 4 to Section 13.
3. See *Savings and Fiscal Privilege* by John Hills, Chapter 6.
4. As footnote 1.
5. If contributions increased in response to a tax on pension fund income, the cost of contribution *relief* would rise, reducing the net revenue gain. See *Taxing Pensions* by V.C. Fry, E.M. Hammond and J.A. Kay (IFS Report Series No.14, 1985).
6. Although it can be argued that, as far as dividends are concerned, the imputation system of Corporation Tax is equivalent to an additional tax on top of Income Tax (see Section 19).
7. See *Prospects for Tax Reform in 1988* by Mervyn King (LSE Financial Markets Group Discussion Paper No.10, 1987).
8. It would, for instance, remove the 'bicycle' effect which might be created with interest deducted at 35% but only taxed at 25%.
9. As they would be losing their newly gained advantage of setting a second allowance against their investment income.

Section 15

1. Figures from *Trends in the Distribution of Wealth in Britain 1923– 1981* by A.B. Atkinson, J. Gordon and A.J. Harrison (TIDI Discussion Paper No.70, London School of Economics, 1986) and *Inland Revenue Statistics 1987*, Table 7.5.
2. The former gives the distribution between individual adults, the latter that between families (tax units).
3. *Economic Trends* November 1987, Table A, p94.
4. Cmnd 7595, paragraph 4.27 (HMSO, 1979).
5. *Trends in the Distribution of Wealth in Britain 1923–1981* by A.B. Atkinson, J. Gordon and A.J. Harrison (TIDI Discussion Paper No.70, London School of Economics, 1986).
6. Figures from *Inland Revenue Statistics 1987*, Tables 7.5–7.7.
7. *Individual Taxes: A Worldwide Summary*, Price Waterhouse, 1988.
8. See *An Annual Wealth Tax* by C.T. Sandford, J.R.M. Willis and D.J. Ironside (Heinemann, 1975).
9. Derived from *Inland Revenue Statistics 1987*, Table 7.5.
10. Ibid, Table 6.5.
11. Quoted in *The Rich Get Richer* by John Rentoul (Unwin Paperbacks, 1987).
12. *Inland Revenue Statistics 1987*, Table 1.1, *Financial Statement and Budget Report 1988–89*, Table 1.2 and equivalents for earlier years.
13. *Hansard* 17 May 1988, Cols WA 423–430.
14. As footnote 12 together with information from *Savings and Fiscal Privilege* by John Hills, Table 3.1.
15. See Chapter 15 of the Meade Committee Report, *The Structure and Reform of Direct Taxation* (George Allen and Unwin, 1978).

Section 16

1. *Financial Statement and Budget Report 1988–89*, Table 1.2.
2. Derived from *Family Expenditure Survey 1986 (Revised)* and based on Figure 6.1 of *Fiscal Harmonisation: An Analysis of the European Commission's Proposals* by Catherine Lee, Mark Pearson and Stephen Smith (IFS Report Series, No.28, 1988).
3. *Economic Trends*, November 1986, Table 3, p101.
4. *Family Expenditure Survey 1979* and *Family Expenditure Survey 1986 (Revised)*.
5. This subsection draws heavily on Lee, Pearson and Smith, op.cit.
6. Calculated from *Family Expenditure Survey 1986 (Revised)* after Lee, Pearson and Smith, op.cit, Table 6.4.
7. See 'Extending the VAT Base: Problems and Possibilities' by Evan Davis and John Kay, *Fiscal Studies*, February 1985.

Section 17

1. Derived from *Economic Trends*, November 1986, Table 5, p107.
2. *Changing Patterns of Smoking: Are There Economic Causes?* by V. Fry and P. Pashardes (IFS Report Series No.30, 1988), Table A1.
3. See *Lectures in Public Economics* by A.B. Atkinson and J.E. Stiglitz (McGraw Hill, 1980), Lecture 12.

4. But note that there are *savings* for the rest of the community from, for instance, the lower amount of pensions which smokers will live to claim.
5. Fry and Pashardes, op.cit.
6. Source: Report of Commissioners of HM Customs and Excise for 1986–87 (HMSO, Cm 238, 1987), Tables D3, E4, F3, G4 and H4. The figures are for 'typical' products, not averages of actual prices.
7. *The British Tax System* by John Kay and Mervyn King, Table 13.1.
8. As footnote 6.
9. This subsection draws heavily on Lee, Pearson and Smith, op.cit.
10. Ibid, Table 6.3.
11. *The Revenue and Welfare Effects of Fiscal Harmonisation for the UK* by Elizabeth Symons and Ian Walker (IFS Working Paper No.88/8).

Section 18

1. *Financial Statement and Budget Report 1988–89*, Table 1.2.
2. See *Local Government Finance: A Practical Guide* by Ian Douglas and Steve Lord (Local Government Information Unit, 1986) for a straightforward description of the current system.
3. 'How far is the Poll Tax a Community Charge? The Implications of Service Usage Evidence' by Glen Bramley, Julian Le Grand and William Low, School of Advanced Urban Studies, University of Bristol, *mimeo*, 1988.
4. See *Paying for Local Government* (HMSO, Cmnd 9714, 1986). For a discussion, see *A Tax on All The People* by Carey Oppenheim (CPAG, 1987).
5. European Community 'harmonisation' of indirect tax rates would also rule it out.
6. See *A Tax on All The People* by Carey Oppenheim (CPAG, 1987), Chapter 4.
7. See *Local Taxes and Local Government* by Stephen Smith and Duncan Squire (IFS Report Series No.25, 1987), Table 5.1.
8. *Administrative Options for a Local Income Tax* by John Kay and Stephen Smith (IFS Commentary, 1987).
9. *The British Tax System* by John Kay and Mervyn King, p150.
10. Derived from Cmnd 9714, Figure F5.
11. These authorities have very large rateable resources (or high spending levels) and did not receive Block Grant at all; they were therefore outside some parts of the equalisation system.
12. This happens because under the old grant system extra resources went to areas with low rateable value per capita. This will no longer happen.
13. It should be remembered, however, that the old system incorporates *reductions* in grant for many authorities if they spend more, but the cost of this is shared between domestic and non-domestic ratepayers.
14. *A Tax on All the People*, Tables G and H, p39.
15. *Local Taxes and Local Government*, p72.
16. The decline in the private rental market and the distortions caused by the mixture of rent control and decontrol means that rental values for domestic property have little meaning. Capital values, by contrast, are readily available from data on sales of owner occupied property.

Section 19

1. See 'On the Growth of Corporation Tax Revenues' by Michael Devereux, *Fiscal Studies*, May 1987.
2. See *Inflation: the Achilles' Heel of Corporation Tax* by John King and Charles Wookey (IFS Report Series No.26, 1987).
3. 'Corporation Tax: the Effect of the 1984 reforms on the Incentive to Invest' by Michael Devereux, *Fiscal Studies*, February 1988.
4. 'The 1984 Corporation Tax Reform' by Jeremy Edwards, *Fiscal Studies*, May 1984.

Section 20

1. A Disability Income Scheme would, for instance, be a desirable component of any reform, but it could not be modelled on TAX-MOD. The details of such a scheme go, in any case, beyond the scope of this book.
2. Approximately 30% of the bottom decile group are unaffected by the reform. These are mostly young adults living with their parents who neither qualify for benefits nor earn enough to pay tax.
3. The reform does not, however, include restoration of Earnings Related Supplement or changes to the principles of Statutory Sick Pay.
4. The impact of this £0.7 billion (and of the extra £0.3 billion from CGT) has been allocated to the top decile group in Figure 20a,

accounting for £6.50 per week of their net losses.
5. The CGT figure is based on the assumption that the typical increase in tax rate would be from 40% to 50% and that overall CGT revenues would be at their 1987–88 level of £1.3 billion (*Inland Revenue Statistics 1987*, Table 1.1).
6. TAXMOD result.

Index

Additional Personal Allowance
for single parents 23,24
Ad valorem taxation
tobacco 7,45
Age allowances 18,27
Alcohol 7,12,44–45
Average rate (income tax) 16
Avoidance 17,24,38

Bank accounts 34,38
Basic income
integration of benefits and tax systems 30,31
Basic rate (income tax) 11,16,18–19
Benefit principle
assessing local taxes 46
Benefits 13,26,28–29,30–32,52–55
Betting duties 44
'Bicycle'
tax avoidance 38
Block Grant 46
Building society accounts 34,38
Buoyancy
rates 46,47
Businesses
See: Companies
Business Expansion Scheme 11,35,38,53

Capitalisation 35
Capital Gains Tax 6,12,33–35,38,41,49,50,54
Capital receipts 41
capital taxes 6
See also: Capital Gains Tax
Capital Transfer Tax
Inheritance Tax
Capital Transfer Tax 6,12,40–41
Car Tax 44–45
Child Benefit 11,30–32
proposals for reform 52–55
Child Tax Allowances 11
Churning 30
Cohabiting couples
See Unmarried couples
Community Charge
See Poll Tax
Companies 39,49–51
Composite rate
tax on bank and building society deposits 34
Comprehensive Income Tax 36–37,38–39
Contingent benefits 32
Corporation Tax 6,34,35,39,49–50
changes since 1979 12
international comparisons 14–15

Death
taxation on death 40–41
Decile groups 10
Depreciation of capital equipment 50
Direct taxes 6,8
See also Income Tax
National Insurance Contributions
Dividends 34,50
Domestic rate relief 46
Domestic rates
See Rates
Double taxation agreements 49

Earnings
average earnings – definition 9
earnings distribution 10,29
– effect of reforming tax system 52–55

Earnings limits
National Insurance Contributions 21
Enterprise zones 11
Equivalent income 10
and Poll Tax 47
Estate Duty 12,41
European Community
harmonisation of excise duties 12,45
harmonisation of Value Added Tax 15,42–43
Evasion 17
Excise duties 7,12,44–45
Exempt goods (Value Added Tax) 42
Exemptions (Income Tax) 18
Expenditure Tax 37,38,39

Factor cost 45
Families
as units of taxation 6
Family Credit 28,29
proposals for reform 52–55
See also Benefits
Fiscal drag 12,13
Forestry
tax concessions 34,35

Gaming duties 44
Gas
See North Sea Revenues
Gearing
spending levels and Poll Tax 48
Gifts
taxes on capital transfers/receipts 41
Gilts 34
Graduated rate structure (income tax) 17,24,53

Harmonisation with European Community
excise duties 12,45
Value Added Tax 14–15,42–43
Higher rate structure (income tax) 16–17,18
Horizontal equity 36
Housing Benefit 28–29,46,48
proposals for reform 52–55
See also Benefits
Husband
See Married Couples
Hybrid tax system 37,38

Imputation system 50
Imputed rent 33
Incidence
who pays the tax 7
who pays the tax on companies 49
Income distribution 8–10
changes since 1979 13
effect of tax allowances 19–20
Income Support 28
proposals for reform 52–55
See also Benefits
Income tax 6,11,16–17
and benefits 13,29,30–32
international comparisons 14–15
and National Insurance Contributions 21–22
personal allowances 18–20
proposals for reform 52–55
Independent taxation 23–24,25–27
See also Married couples
Indirect taxes 6,55
effect on income 8–9
international comparison 14–15
See also Excise duties
Value Added Tax
Inheritance Tax 6,12,40–41,55
Integration
of Income Tax and benefits 30–31
of Income Tax and National Insurance Contributions 22
International comparisons
Income Tax 14–15
taxation of married couples 25
wealth tax 40
Investment income 33–35,36–37,38–39
taxation of married couples 23–24
Investment Income Surcharge 11,33
proposals for reform 38–39,53

Joint taxation
    See Married couples

Life Assurance 34
Life Assurance Premium Relief 34,38,53
Lifetime Accessions Tax 41
Local income tax 46–48,55
    countries administering local income tax 14–15
Local sales tax 47

Marginal rate (Income Tax) 16,18
Married couples 23–24, 25–27
    capital gains 35
    investment income 38–39
Married Couple's Allowance (from 1990) 23,24,26–27
    proposals for reform 54–55
Married Man's Allowance 18,23,26–27
    proposals for reform 54–55
Means-tested benefits
    See Benefits
MIRAS
    See mortgage relief
Mortgage relief 35,38
    Mortgage Interest Relief At Source (MIRAS) 18
    £30,000 limit 24,33
    proposals for reform 53
Multi-national corporations 14
    See also Companies

1992 42–43
National insurance benefits
    See Benefits
National Insurance Contributions 6,11–12,38–39
    paid by employees 21–22
    paid by employers 49,50–51
    reform proposals 52–55
    self-employed 51
National Insurance Surcharge 12
National savings 34
Negative income tax 31
Neutral tax system
    reform of taxation on investment income 37
NICs
    See National Insurance Contributions
Non-domestic rates 46,47,48,49,51
North Sea Revenues 12,49

Oil
    See North Sea Revenues
Owner occupation
    imputed rent 33
    See also Mortgage relief

Pay As You Earn (P.A.Y.E.) 6
Pensioners
    age allowance 18
    married couples – taxation from 1990 24,27
    reforms of tax of investment income 38–39
    See also Pensions
Pensions
    private pension funds 33–34,35,53
    – tax free lump sums 38
    state pensions – proposals for reform 52–55
Personal allowances 11,16–17,18–20
    fiscal drag 12
    married couples 23–24,25–27
    proposals for reform 30–32,52–55
Personal equity plans 11,35
Personal pension schemes 35
    See also Pensions
Petrol 7,12,44–45
Poll Tax 7,11,33,46–48,55
Poverty trap 29,31–32
Progressive taxation 7,8
    excise duties 44
    Income Tax 17,18
    rates 46
    Value Added Tax 42
Property Tax
    See Rates
Proportional taxation 8,21

Quintile groups 8–9

Rateable value 46
Rate poundage 46
Rate rebate
    See Housing Benefit
Rates 6–7,11,12,33,46–48,55
Rate Support Grant 46
Realisation of capital gains 35
Regressive taxation 8,21
Rents
    tax on land and commercial property 34
Retail Price Index 9
Revenue Support Grant 46,47

Sales taxes
    local sales taxes 47
    See also Value Added Tax
SERPS
    See State Earnings Related Pension Scheme
Share options 11,35,38,53
Shares 34,50
Single parents
    Additional Personal Allowance 23,24
Social dividend
    integration of benefits and tax systems 30–32
Standard rated goods (Value Added Tax) 42
State Earnings Related Pension Scheme 21
Stock relief 49–50

Take-up of benefits 28
Tapering of benefits 28
Targeting of benefits 30–31
Taxable income 9–10,16
Tax base 14
Tax credit system 18–19,32
Tax cuts 11–13,29
Taxmod 5,52–55
Tax reliefs 18–20
    See also Mortgage relief
              Pensions
              Life Assurance Premium Relief
Tax return 6
Tax schedule 25
Tax system
    changes since 1979 11–13
    international comparisons 14–15
    reform proposals 52–55
Tax unit 6
Tobacco 7,12,44–45,55
Transferable allowances
    between married couples 25
Transfer pricing
    manipulation of pricing by multi-national corporations 14
Trusts 35

Uniform Business Rate 46,47,48,51
Unit Trusts 34
Universalism
    of benefits 28
Unmarried couples
    Additional Personal Allowance for children 23,24
    mortgage relief 24

Value Added Tax (VAT) 6,42–43,55
    changes since 1979 12
    and excise duties 44–45
    harmonisation with European Community 14–15,42–43
Vanishing exemptions 18
VAT
    See Value Added Tax

Vehicle Excise Duty 44–45
Vertical equity 36

Wealth tax 40–41,55
Wife
    See Married couples
Wife's earned income allowance 18,23
Wife's Earning Election 23

Zero Rate Band (Income Tax) 19
Zero rated goods (Value Added Tax) 42